D1565475

A VILLAGE WEDDING

The Bride's Herbal

Weddings and Other Parties

by Bertha Reppert

A Handbook Helpful for The Bride, Her Family and Friends

proffering Joy and Beauty for
- Weddings
- Receptions
- Showers
- Anniversaries

including
- 100 Herbal Recipes, Favors, Decorations and Crafts

augmented by the
- Timeless Symbolism of Herbs

First Printing 1989

ISBN 0-9617210-3-0

Published by
Remembrance Press
120 S. Market Street
Mechanicsburg, PA 17055

and to

ALL BRIDES who know that in matters of
The HEART and The HEARTH

"Herbs Make the Difference"

Thank you note

I SEEM ALWAYS BEHOLDEN to good friends and loving family who pitch in to help on my many projects. This book is no exception. Besides hugs and kisses to Byron, my patient helpmate of four decades plus, I am so very grateful to Rosina, Frances, several Helen's, Vicki, Gary, Colleen, Susanna, Katy, Sharon, Holly, Nancy, Minga, Theresa, Marjorie, Carol, Carolynn, Scott, Hildegard, Emily and a host of others who shall be nameless, even to me. Who knows the origin of a great! idea or recipe? This little herbal handbook for brides is built on a pyramid of such inspiration as well as the bounty from my herb garden.

And a special thanks to all the brides who allowed me to be a part of their weddings. To the best of my knowledge all the knots are still tied and herbs deserve a lot of the credit.

XXOO
Bertha

TABLE OF CONTENTS

HERBS MAKE THE DIFFERENCE

This is the Wedding Portrait of Ottylie Elgert and Gustav Peplau who were Wed February 12, 1907

Cover, portrait, and artwork by Artist Granddaughter Marjorie Louise Reppert

HERBS AND THE WEDDING PLANS

Every part of the happy preparations for a wedding can — indeed should — include herbs. Be it a simple ceremony before the fireplace at home or an elaborate processional in a lofty cathedral, include fragrant symbolic herbs in as many ways as possible. The scent and beauty and symbolism of herbs make them most suitable to wedding plans. Let this book help you choose some of the ways.

HERBS MAKE THE DIFFERENCE FOR BRIDES

You can use herbs in general — fresh, dried, or pressed — in any quantity available to you. If you have an herb garden, that's splendid; but if not, don't let that stop you from planning an herbal wedding. Perhaps they can be purchased somewhere in your area. Try farmers' markets (ask for bunches of sage, mint, and other common herbs, then place an order), local gardeners, members of garden clubs, herb or health food shops, yes, even supermarkets.***

You can do a lot with readily available bunches of parsley or the dried herbs and spices sold in bottles and tins for seasoning. Sometimes cooperative florists can get you the herbs you are seeking, especially fresh bay, rosemary, or myrtle, which may have to be flown in from warmer climates.

A sure source of fresh herbs can be found in the back of this book. These are reputable herb growers who know how to condition and pack fresh herbs for shipping. Write and request prices. Rest assured that for this once-in-a-lifetime event that will be the "talk of the town" fresh herbs flown in are well worth their price.

Remember though, that central to all this for a truly memorable wedding, is the use of herbs. Let herbs do all the work for you — help you lay your plans and pleasantly see them through to a most satisfactory conclusion. Your plans co-ordinated around a color harmony, a collection of your "favorite things," and herbs will insure your wedding will linger in everyone's memory for years. Unto the next generation. Believe me!

---

* Indicates the recipe is included. See Recipe Index.

** Instructions are included in the Crafts section.

*** See Sources.

CHOOSING A THEME AND COLORS

Whether you are putting together a new costume, redecorating a room, planning your Christmas decorations or setting up a year's program for a successful club, it is best and most easily accomplished with a theme. In orchestrating your wedding — from announcements to thank you notes — a theme is your salvation. LET HERBS BE YOUR SPECIAL THREAD WOVEN THROUGH ALL THE FESTIVITIES AND FORMALITIES, tying everything together.

It also helps to choose a color harmony. This could be the bride's favorite colors (blue, pink, or purple), or dictated by the season (fall colors; garnet and off-white for Christmas), or the choice of the wedding party (pink and white) or pastels, or something terribly old and now considered smartly modern, an "all white" wedding. Make your choice then stick to it; coordinate all your plans around these colors. Once the decision is made, many tasks are easier and the total impact will be smashing.

If you collect stuffed teddy bears or adore roses, have shelves of English cottages, think butterflies are the loveliest of God's creations or can't resist antique baskets, have a collection of dolls from around the world or enjoy seashells, incorporate your natural proclivity into your plans. "Favorite things" make a most charming theme — especially when combined with herbs.

Once you have chosen a color and a favorite thing to use as your theme, it is also possible to limit your choice of herbs to just one such as rosemary for "remembrance" or to three such as parsley, sage, and angelica, or my preference, to use an assortment of herbs.

If you choose to use just parsley as your herbal theme, you will be amazed at the many ways it can be incorporated. Have you ever looked closely at a bunch of parsley? A brilliant dark green curled into ruffled convolutions, glowing with health, it symbolizes "victory." Parsley mixes beautifully with wedding flowers, can be used in centerpieces as well as a lavish garnish. Tuck it into invitations, announcements, and thank you notes and, when silvered or gilded***, makes stunning jewelry gifts for the bridesmaids and groomsmen.

THE ANNOUNCEMENT

When a betrothed couple makes their family and friends aware of their future plans together, it can be a large social gathering, a tea party, a luncheon with the girls, or a simple announcement of intentions. Name a date — not more than a year ahead, please — if you want people to plan to join in your festivities. Any of the party suggestions in this book, the herbs and the recipes* in the back section can be incorporated into an announcement gala.

Today the lady usually shows her friends her engagement ring and that is the symbol of one's betrothal promise. If you are in an office or belong to a big family or participate in the activities of a rather good sized church congregation, you might consider setting your herbal theme right at the start.

Rosemary — "that's for remembrance" — is a symbolic gesture. Distribute little sprigs of the herb, tied with ribbons, and a small white card with your name and his name and the date. If plants of rosemary are not available or not of sufficient size to supply many sprigs, attach to the card tiny packets of whole dried rosemary from your spice cupboard.

Myrtle has been symbolic of love and the emblem of marriage for centuries. Hand out little sprigs of fragrant myrtle, the true *Myrtus communis* of Biblical times, tied with small white bows, as a unique announcement. Attach your engagement message, printed or handwritten.

Furthermore, for those living far away, an announcement note containing your rosemary or myrtle sprig travels well in the mail.

Engagement parties and showers will provide the most ways to utilize the unique powers of these simple plants. They can be used in the invitation, as favors, as centerpieces to decorate the food table, in corsages for the mothers of the bride- and groom-to-be, and in the menu, especially in the herbal punch*. Be prepared to distribute copies of the recipes to all in attendance because they will be intrigued by your herbal refreshments. Perhaps these can be favors, again repeating the names of the happy couple and the date of the wedding to come.

If, perchance, you are a part of a large lunchroom gathering, such as an office or school faculty cafeteria, a tray of heart-shaped herb cookies decorated with both your initials and a small standing announcement will provide the excitement for that day. Because caraway seeds were once given to engaged couples to keep them from straying — it is said to confer the "gift of retention" — use the recipe for caraway cookies* in the back of this book.

THE TETE-A-TETE

Moonlight and roses, candlelight and wine, soft music and a well planned, easy-but-elegant menu is the time to plot your wedding plans and tell him all about the romance and magic of herbs.

Gain your betrothed's full cooperation on this lest your all-herbal wedding plans go awry. He should know your wishes and enjoy going along with the fun.

Serve an herb soup* and use herbs liberally in the salad with edible flower garnishes. Rosemary wine* would go nicely with such a menu and a centerpiece of simple parsley, if that's all that's available, will help the conversation flow the way you want.

Surely this little book will suggest many creative ways to share your rightful place in the spotlight with herbs. Indeed, there are enough ideas for several prospective new households! Pick and choose the ones that suit your lifestyle best. Build upon the suggestions and improvise too.

With the strains of "Lohengrin" in the background, you will plan a truly special event and the herbs will make it more so. Be sure your intended understands. He will soon join you in the delights and pleasures of herbs.

WEDDINGS AND OTHER PARTIES

A WELL HERBED WEDDING

Recently, a local wedding was made doubly memorable by the inventive use of herbs. Everyone privileged to attend will long remember the beauty and symbolism present at this charming ceremony.

The theme was created by using green rosemary (for remembrance), gray lavender (for luck), and blue rue (the herb of grace), throughout the festivities. The bride carried these three herbs with a single large white rose (symbol of love), baby's breath, and a bit of pearly everlasting (for constancy) attached to a potpourri bag made of organdy eyelet trimmed with antique beaded lace and satin ribbons to match her off-white gown. The bag carried by the bride was the size of a muff, supported by ribbons on the back, creating a most unusual accessory.

In the fragrant potpourri bag was a special blend of more symbolic herbs: violet leaves (modesty and simplicity), mullein (once used in love potions), lamb's ears (for soft caresses), basil (symbol of courtship), sage (for good health and domestic tranquility), linden blossoms (for beauty, grace, and simplicity, "the qualities of the perfect wife"), along with the thematic lavender, rue, and rosemary, plus rosebuds. It was a sentimental concoction of heavenly fragrance.

The combined lavender, rosemary, and rue became the groomsmen boutonnieres as well as enhancing all the special ladies' orchid corsages. Tiny sprigs of the same tri-herbal combination graced the halo worn by the bride. Little sweetheart roses, baby's breath, and more white pearly everlasting created an enchanting hairpiece.

A single long stemmed pink rose caught with the very same wedding herbs was carried by each bridesmaid, who also wore a headband similar to the bride's halo.

Two little girls, nieces of the bride, carried tussie-mussies, small nosegays of dried rosebuds, fragrant cloves (for dignity), parsley (emblem of victory), and more rosemary glued onto a lacy white paper doily. These were easily made well in advance and were kept for years after.

For a touch of whimsey, a pinch of caraway seeds was tucked into the groom's breast pocket. Because it confers the gift of retention, caraway was believed to be given the power to keep husbands from straying.

Among the gifts was a basket of herb plants to start a new little kitchen garden. It contained a romanwood plant (for constancy and perseverance), a rosemary plant (sacred to weddings), and a packet of lunaria seeds. Known as "silver dollars" or "money plant." Lunaria symbolizes "money in all pockets" and was customarily given to newlyweds to plant in their garden because it was believed it would keep the happy household from want. The rosemary plant will prove the test of the marriage for 'tis said that rosemary "grows only where the mistress is master!"

Naturally the wedding cake was equally adorned. Asters in the shades of the wedding party gowns, flowers from the bride's grandmother's garden, and snippets of the same lavender, rosemary, and rue topped the traditional tiered cake. Hawaiian wedding cakes* on either side were decorated with chartreuse lemon balm leaves (for comfort), a perfect compliment to the colors and flavors in this delectable recipe.

Centering the wedding party table was a garland of grayed artemisias, silver-like in the moonlight and symbolic of dignity, combined with pink "Fairy Roses," dried so that the happy bride and groom could take it to their new home to use as a doorpiece. The fragrant potpourri bag with all of the wedding herbs will become an heirloom sachet tucked into a bureau drawer as a joyous and treasured reminder of this memorable day.

All the emotions and feelings we would like to express on such an occasion have been caught up in the symbolism of these gentle herbs, speaking with an eloquence all their own. From hence forth, perhaps, the legendary magic of rosemary, lavender, and rue in company with all the others will continue to work their spell on the young couple in mysterious ways. Who can say?

TEA AND TUSSIE-MUSSIES

Celebrating a Royal Wedding is an unaccustomed treat for Americans. Since the whole world was invited — via satellite television — to the once-in-a-lifetime grand occasion, we had the fun of sharing the pomp and circumstance of a glorious day. So romantic!

Liveried footmen in pink stockings, a glass coach with a real fairytale Princess dressed in English gossamer, a handsome Prince announced by blaring trumpeteers, and bells that peeled for four hours in a sequence of 5,000 different combinations is unforgettable. How wonderful to participate, however remotely.

Here in Mechanicsburg, far from the press of London crowds, we invited all who wished to share in the fun to "tea with tussie-mussies." We entertained on our porch.

An oversized table of boards and sawhorses was set up on the freshly swept and re-organized side porch. Dressed with a queen-sized lavender sheet topped with our best polyester lace, our old porch has never looked so festive. A bouffant bouquet of wedding-like Queen Ann's Lace from a nearby field was surrounded by low bowls of small tussie-mussies, a myriad of casual bunches, and colorful bows. These became our favors for all attending, ladies and gentlemen.

At the end of our long table were beribboned baskets of English lavender sachets, additional souvenirs for guests. At the opposite end of the table was a large punch bowl, afloat with herbs and flowers as garnish. Royal Wedding Punch* was a hit, one gentleman savoring his, sipping and sniffing it like fine wine.

Along with the tea/punch, we served rose petal sandwiches*, lemon balm jelly* on tiny salted crackers, and little herbwiches* we called "Lady Di's Diamonds"*. Candied violets* and other herbal sweetmeats graced the table, nibbles to munch while signing the guest register with messages for the Prince of Wales and his new Princess.

The wedding music from St. Paul's, repeated on public radio, was a magnificent background. One perfect day, even with "maximum mugginess," such as the one we enjoyed with their Royal Highnesses, restores hope to a world grown weary and helps keep each of us young.

English in origin, the tussie-mussies (little nosegays of herbs and "lovesome flowers") were the hit of the party. Decorations, conversation pieces, and gay little favors all in one, they saw our delighted guests on their way home — fragrantly.

"Tea and Tussie-Mussies," or the way we celebrated the Royal Wedding, is an easy herbal party suitable for an "at home" or "open house" given for or by the newlyweds.

TUSSIE-MUSSIES

A Tussie-Mussie is Medieval in origin. It is a bouquet of sweet smelling herbs which was often carried by ladies.

Queen Elizabeth was presented with one at her coronation in Westminster Abbey, as a symbol of her high rank.

Tussie-Mussies include fragrant herbs as well as symbolic herbs

Roses for Love
Artemisias for Constancy
Mint for Joy
Lavender for Luck
Sage for Good Health
Thyme for Courage
Lemon Balm for Comfort
and
"Rosemary, that's for Remembrance"

You may keep your Tussie-Mussie fresh for a week in water, then allow it to dry to last forever.

Made especially for you.

WHENEVER . . .
There's something special
. . . and someone special
PRESENT A TUSSIE-MUSSIE . . .
An old fashioned nosegay,
sweet with fragrant fresh herbs,
beribboned in sentiment,
steeped in symbolism.
IT'S PERFECT . . .
For that someone special
on that special occasion.

Tussie-Mussies, fresh or dried, large or small, formal rounds or simple bunches, become a timeless theme for an herbal wedding. We made forty-six for one wonderful affair! When presented, we also give a copy of the above inscription. Symbolism, history, and care all in one, you may photocopy it for your own use.

A BRIDAL PARTY "AL FRESCO" A LA HERBES

To announce the impending event, to shower the bride, or to greet the newly married couple, entertain outdoors weather permitting. Everyone loves a picnic so why not? But make this a picnic with a difference — serve an elegant menu *a la herbes*.

Select burlap cloths and pottery or checkered tablecloths and paper plates or no-iron terry cloth and melamine — or go all out and use linen and china. Prancing down the center of the tables, have a large number of matched green mineral water bottles. Gather an assortment of gay garden flowers and herbs, placing one or two in each bottle. What centerpiece could be easier? Or more effective? Or as charming?

For favors, have a palm leaf fan for each guest to which you have attached a bunch of basil and lemon balm with a pretty ribbon. As they fan the warm air, the herbs will make it fragrant while keeping away flies and gnats.

When it is time for your guests to move towards the picnic area, give each one a hobo stick with a colorful man's work handkerchief, corners knotted over the stick or twig, containing the utensils and soft dinner rolls filled with shrimp salad.

To go with this, you might consider the following beautiful, delicious, and well herbed menu:

Blueberry Soup*
Salad a Fleur*
Dip with Crudites*
Fruit Skewers*
Iced Herb Tea*

Additional favors could be little hobo stick sachets to match the picnic. Make them on pipe cleaners or small twigs.

A PROGRESSIVE DINNER PARTY

In a close knit family or extremely compatible neighborhood, a travelling party is a fun way to entertain. Each course from soup to nuts is served at a different house, each hostess featuring a different herb, decor, dish, or favor.

This can be three houses or twelve, depending upon your inspiration and cooperation and enthusiasm. One impromptu committee meeting should divide the work so that everyone enjoys the party.

Add the recipes and dried herbs used at each party stop to a recipe box and spice rack presented to the bride-to-be along with the dessert. Gifts can be centerpieces, opened in small batches at each stop as the party progresses.

A ROSEMARY WEDDING – "THAT'S FOR REMEMBRANCE"

I'm sure the very first wedding bouquets, centuries ago, included rosemary. Ancient symbol of remembrance, it also signifies devotion and loyalty. Its fragrance and association with matters of the head and heart make rosemary ideally suited to weddings. Indeed, it is THE herb of weddings.

In Yugoslavia, rosemary is given to all the wedding guests as they enter the church when it is pinned on the lapel to be worn throughout the festivities.

In merry old England, where the strewing of fresh rose petals is still traditional at weddings, the sprigs of rosemary were gilded and then distributed to the guests.

Because rosemary is symbolic of love and loyalty, English bridesmaids of years gone by presented the bridegroom with a bunch of it on his wedding morning. Wouldn't today's groom be astounded by such a ceremony? A sprig of rosemary was always included in the bridal bouquet, thus to insure happiness and good luck. Branches of rosemary were used as well to decorate the halls and churches during the wedding and burned as incense during the religious service.

In Mexico, rosemary is grown as a good luck charm. Referred to as "she," the plant is tended as protection against witches and their deviltry. A recent exchange student says she was given pieces from the sacred rosemary plant to pack in her luggage for a safe return journey home by train. However, a companion didn't get any for her trip home because she was flying and since witches don't travel on planes, the family considered it unnecessary. Be sure to pack rosemary in your going-away suitcase!

"Speaking of the powers of rosemary . . .
it overtoppeth all the flowers in the garden."

Indeed, pots of rosemary could glorify a wedding, if available. Line the steps of the church, edge the aisle and ornament the chancel, decorate the reception hall and use them as favors. Such a wedding reaps special blessings.

Rosemary is for remembrance
Between us day and night.
Wishing that I might always have
You present in my sight.

Thomas Robinson, **A Nosegay for Lovers** (1584)

ROSEMARY'S WEDDING

"There's rosemary, that's for remembrance;
— there's rue for you; and here's some for me;
we may call it, herb o' grace o' Sundays —"

Shakespeare

When a girl named Rosemary whose initials happened to be R.U.E. got married, guess her herbal theme! Right. Lots of rosemary, for remembrance, and rue, Shakespeare's herb of grace.

Because the wedding was in the dead of Winter, we elected to dry a great deal of rosemary, rue "Blue Beauty," lavender for luck, as well as many other herbs and a host of little "Fairy" roses to create a nosegay bouquet and halo** for the bride and bridesmaids — bouquets from the Summer harvest.

Using moss covered floral foam and lace doilies, the fragile herbs and flowers along with a cloud of fresh baby's breath and a host of ribbons were easily transformed into many wedding arrangements.

After the ceremony, they were enjoyed as dried decorations for many years, treasured keepsakes still speaking their herbal messages eloquently, "to have and to hold" forever.

Love note *Using the sources in the back of this book, today's Winter bride can order all the fresh herbs she wants from growers equipped to cut, condition, and ship fresh herbs, second day air, twelve months of the year.*

LOTS O' LACE WEDDING

Nostalgia, sentiment, old-fashioned traditions — if this is your dream of a wedding, do it with lace. Buy yards and yards of lacy-look material and a bolt of 3" lace to use on everything. Seek out lace-like paper napkins, lacy invitations, paper doilies and everything else you can think of to utilize. Grandmother's old fashioned laces are treasures to use.

HERE ARE A FEW IDEAS: Make simple squares of lace to cover tops of tables; stitch up small lace pouches to fill with potpourri as favors at a party; 6" squares of lace will make lovely sachet favors with no sewing; carry a lace bedecked nosegay — perhaps tied to a lacy parasol; glue a bit of lace on one side of the invitation; wrap the bridesmaids gifts in lace-look paper; use paper doilies under everything including the candles and centerpieces; tuck it into the bouquets and the wreaths on the door; make a lavishly laced ring pillow; wear lace, of course. Your wedding will be very special and beautiful beyond words, from announcements to thank you notes, if you lace it lavishly.

LACY THANK YOU CARDS: Buy plain notepapers and matching envelopes. Cut a lace heart out of paper or cloth and glue it on the front. Use white glue thinned with an equal amount of water. When the glue is dried — don't lay them on top of each other! — press your note papers flat with a warm iron and proceed to write your thank you's.

LACY NOSEGAYS: This is an easy sit-down Summer-Fall project best accomplished while fresh herbs and dried flowers are available in abundance. Cut 18" pieces of 2" or 3" wide lace and, with easy running stitches, gather one side and pull into a circle. Overcast the seam. This takes a few minutes for each nosegay. Put together little bunches of herbs, seed pods, colorful dried flowers, and baby's breath. Secure the little bunch with a rubber band and poke through the center of the lacy circle. Ribbons may be added if you wish. Wrap the stems with white florist tape. Easiest to work with while fresh, the herbs will dry in place, creating a fragrant nosegay. Pile them on a pedestal cake plate — or tiered cake plates — for centerpieces that are also favors. They are truly a "thing of beauty" laying on the branches of a Christmas tree. Add small gold balls.

NATURE'S LACE: In Summer, gather all the snowy Queen-Ann's-lace you can find. Reduce the stems to 2" or so. Promptly place in a shoe box of sterilized playbox sand (available at any hardware store or builder's supply place). Have an inch of sand in the bottom. Lay the Queen Ann's lace blossoms head down, stem up. Cover completely with more sand. In about a week, your beautiful lacy blossoms will be permanently dried, to use as decorations or to be glued on invitations. Spray them with hair spray (a touch of glitter may be added for a holiday mood) and pack them away in plastic covered boxes, safe from the summer's humidity, until needed. They have a fairyland quality when used to decorate wreaths or a Christmas tree or in bridal bouquets.

Is this the little girl I carried?
Is this the little boy at play?
I don't remember getting older;
When did they?

— Fiddler on the Roof

DO YOU KNOW A FIELD OF DAISIES?

He loves me,
He loves me not,
He loves me,
He loves me not,
He loves me . .

"Daisy, Daisy, give me your answer true!" Delight in daisies in May! If you know where there is a meadow filled with daisies, plan to put them into your wedding. Symbol of innocence, Wordsworth's "bright flowers" are a lovely theme for a wedding and all the pre-nuptial parties.

Use them lavishly, by the basketfull, and don't overlook traditional daisy chains, garlands of long stemmed daisies tied together in a thick rope. Secure them with stout carpet thread or crochet cotton and keep them in plastic bags under refrigeration until needed. Then wrap them artistically using a bolt of narrow satin ribbon. Any extra ribbon can be made into bows for the chain.

Make your daisy chains in several continuous lengths to be used to crown the bride, to mark pews at the church, a long section to lay along the edge of the head table at the reception, around the punch bowl and the wedding cake. The bridesmaids, like a Kate Greenaway print, can carry the chains instead of bouquets and the flower girl can start the proceedings by strewing a few daisy flowers in the bride's path.

If every guest is presented with a long stemmed field daisy, you could have a symbolic "tying of the knot." At a given point in the ceremony, all daisies are simply tied to each other. Florist flowers have stiff stems; however, the wild flowers have supple stems and so it's easier to do it with them.

As the ushers, wearing daisy boutonnieres, empty the church, they should be instructed to collect the single daisy chain to decorate the reception hall.

Everyone loves "the eye of the day"! "Day's eyes" are an appealing symbol-theme to carry throughout all the wedding plans. Use them in every way imaginable . . . altar flowers, mother's corsages, on your thank you notes. Be sure to press some to frame with your invitation for they express "loyal love."

Daisy mums are available all year from the florist, as are silk flower daisies for pre-May festivities.

MELISSA'S WEDDING

Every little girl named Melissa has a built-in theme with her very own herb — lemon balm or *Melissa officinalis.* The chartreuse foliage in baskets combines richly with field daisies in May or with gold roses in June or mums at anytime. The theme of such a wedding should be:

1. Yellow and white (color theme)
2. Baskets (favorite things theme)
3. Lemon balm (herb theme)

Melissa can press the leaves to use on her notes; make a tea with the herb; serve it with ginger ale for a party punch*; add lemon sherbet to make it more festive; or add champagne or sherry for the wedding punch, a true Melissa gala.

Melissa is a prolific herb. A few plants of it will dress tables; provide decorations for around the cake (especially with Hawaiian Wedding Cake*); and huge bouquets for the entire wedding party. Melissa's Jelly* will make delightful favors at a party.

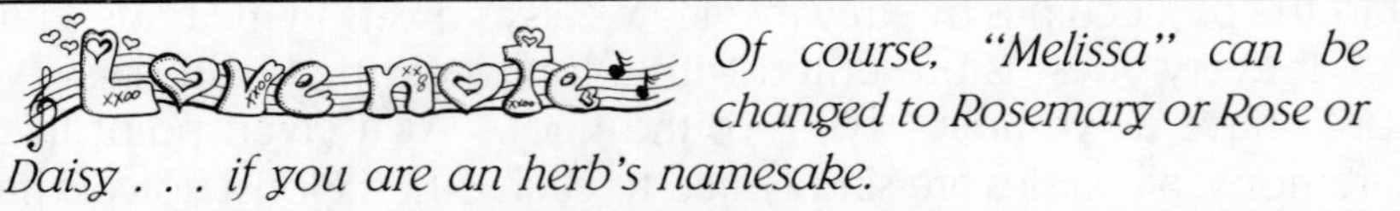

Of course, "Melissa" can be changed to Rosemary or Rose or Daisy . . . if you are an herb's namesake.

Balm was the main ingredient of the celebrated Carmelite Water, made by the nuns at the abbey of St. Juste six hundred years ago. This became an important addition to the toilet preparations of cultured men and women in Mediaeval Europe. It is made from 2 pounds of fresh balm leaves; 1/4 pound of lemon peel; 2 ounces each of nutmeg, cloves, and coriander, a little cinnamon, and some angelica root. These are placed in a still together with 1/2 gallon of orange-flower water and 1 gallon of alcohol and slowly distilled. The "London Dispensatory" of 1696 said that it would "renew youth" and it was also taken as a restorative cordial.

Pliny and, later, Gerard, recommended rubbing balm leaves on a new hive to make the bees stay and balm tea was taken by countrymen as a tonic. Culpeper said "it causes the mind and the heart to become merrie." Due to the presence of potassium salts, it is a valuable restorative and gives one a sense of well being.

The chopped leaves make a pleasing addition to a cream cheese sandwich or, used sparingly, to a salad; they act in the same way as borage when placed in summer drinks.

Taken from **Flowers and Herbs of Love** by Roy Genders

**"She comes! Oh birds, to hail your queen combine,
With pipes and trills and wanderings mazy,
Singing — all Nature loves thee,
Queen White Daisy."**
— Thomas Hood

"THE SECOND WEDDING"

A charming couple we know said their vows with herbs at a simple home wedding. At this joyous union of two good sized families, the bride carried a flat basket of little herbal nosegays surrounding one larger bouquet which she treasures as a keepsake. A second similar basket of nosegays dressed the buffet table as a centerpiece. All together, there were 40 little fragrant tussie-mussies, gay with green, lavender, and yellow ribbon streamers, one for each of the guests and family members in attendance. After the party was over, they were distributed for each guest to take home as a fragrant symbolic remembrance.

For this very special occasion, the bride chose the following herbs, a sprig of each for every little nosegay. The symbolism was hand-written on small white cards by several of the older children:

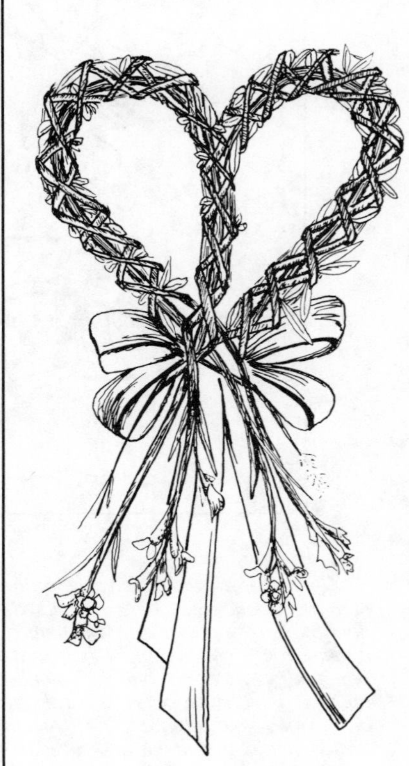

A Small Fragrant Favor

1. Make 2 braids using 6 spikes of fresh lavender.
2. Form 2 loops with flower heads hanging down.
3. Tie with bow.

"Lavender for Luck"

Mint for Joy
Lavender for Luck
Lemon Balm for Comfort
Southernwood for Fun and Fragrance
A Rose for Love
and
Rosemary for Remembrance.

HERB BOUQUETS: Gather your herbs, mint, lemon balm, roses, southernwood, and so forth, a sprig of each for each bouquet. Condition them and keep them in water as long as possible before putting the little bouquets together. (See page 47.) Gathering a sprig of each of the herbs together in one informal bunch, secure the stems with twine or a rubber band. Cover stems with florist tape or foil and affix a bow, with or without streamers. Place them in a flat basket. Keep under refrigeration wrapped in plastic until the last possible moment so they remain well conditioned throughout the festivities.

IDEAS FOR AN HERBAL KITCHEN SHOWER

THEME: Use herbs, in abundance, and a pretty color scheme too. Don't forget to include some of your favorite things — baskets, your doll collection, antiques, or an assortment of hearts to help set the stage.

INVITATIONS: Hand written or purchased, glue on pressed herbs or dried spices. Ask each person to bring along a favorite recipe and the main seasoning ingredient to go with it. Supply the bride-to-be with a recipe file, a spice cupboard or a pretty basket to receive these special personalized herbal goodies, something to put them in to be taken to their new homestead.

CENTERPIECE: Group many "things herbal" in the center of the table or buffet. For instance, pots or bunches of herbs, dried herbs in apothecary jars, a cook book, glass jars or bowls of pretty potpourri, scented candles, a mortar and pestle, whole spices, a kitchen towel with herbs on it, and so forth. They make a charming grouping, like the cover of your favorite herbal, especially when placed on a wooden board or in a flat basket. Sometimes these can be from the hostess's collection or they can be additional herbal gifts to be given to the honored guest. Incorporate your "favorite things" too, of course.

GIFTS: Kitchen gadgets, herbal things, or whatever the bride needs. A spice trousseau (see page 35) is nice to consider.

FAVORS:

1. Herb charts rolled into a scroll with a bag of parsley, sage, rosemary, or thyme. Tie with a bow in your color scheme.
2. A recipe served at the party, written on a card with a tablespoon of the main seasoning ingredient attached in a small envelope.
3. Spice posies** — spices glued with dried flowers in a white doily and finished with ribbons. Charming! Fragrant! Easy!
4. A nosegay of fresh herbs with symbolism attached — marjoram for joy, thyme for courage, rosemary for remembrance, and so on — all tied with ribbons and laces.
5. A small bottle of your favorite seasoned salt, herb jelly, or homemade tarragon vinegar for each guest.
6. A packet of herb seeds to grow in one's own garden is always popular, especially if it is a gift from your garden to theirs. Be sure the bride-to-be receives a pack of each kind you distribute.
7. Little pots of herbs. These can be placed in the center of the table as your decoration, too. Label each one.
8. An old fashioned nutmeg grater and nutmeg tied with ribbons in the party colors.
9. A whole long cinnamon stick with the recipe for mulled cider* attached.
10. Small sacks or sachets of wedding rice** — rice with rosemary "for remembrance" and roses "for love" — to be used at the wedding.

MENU: Advance planning is the secret. Have herbal sandwiches, an herbal dip, spicy cake or cookies, and edible flowers* too, as a garnish or to eat. There are so many good things to serve that include herbs and spices. By all means, serve a good herb tea — peppermint, rosehip, camomile, whatever you think your guests will enjoy, hot or cold, iced or spiced. Herb tea is always a hit at a party. "Constant Comment," a purchased tea by Bigelow, is especially good. It's fun, too, to put an attractive basket of assorted herb tea bags on the party tea tray. Some guests will try more than one kind.

**Indicates directions will be found under "Herbal Wedding Crafts" or see Index.

EXTRAS: Do use herbal napkins. Be sure to garnish liberally with herbs and colorful edible flowers (unsprayed). Bouquets of fragrant herbs throughout the house, especially in the powder room, and a dried herbal wreath on the door add to the ambience charmingly. Greet the guest of honor with an herbal tussie-mussie.

The Rosemary House has a good collection of over twenty herb tea parties with themes. Recipe booklets available include dips, sandwiches, cakes, cookies, and the herb tea to serve if you need additional suggestions. We also carry herb napkins, spice charts, fresh herbs in summer, and all "things herbal." It's your one stop herb shop.

THE NEWLYWEDS' SPICE CABINET

To stock a proper seasoning shelf, gather together at least the following supplies, either fresh and dried from the garden (the best) or purchased in matched bottles. To preserve the flavor, be sure they are stored away from heat, light, and humidity. A spice chart or two would go well with this trousseau of seasonings.

Anise
Basil
Bay leaves: whole and powdered
Cayenne pepper
Chili powder
Cinnamon: sticks and powdered
Cloves: whole and powdered
Curry powder
Dill: seed and weed
Fennel: whole
Garlic: powder, chips or salt
Ginger: ground
Marjoram
Mint
Mustard powder

Nutmeg: whole with a grater
Onion: powder, salt, and flakes
Oregano
Parsley
Paprika
Pepper: whole with a grinder
Poppy seed
Sesame seed
Sage: rubbed
Seasoned salt(s)
Soy sauce
Tabasco sauce
Tarragon
Worcestershire sauce

This list can go on and on, ad infinitum, but it's a beginning. Cardamon, saffron, juniper berries, and cilantro can be added later — or perhaps never. It can also represent a good sized investment for newlyweds. Consider a spice shower where friends contribute the necessities to fill a handsome spice cabinet with tried-and-true recipes to get the couple off on the right track.

CANDLES AND CANDLELIGHT

A late afternoon or an evening wedding in a darkened church is magnificent and allows maximum usage of candlelight.

Visit the church at the approximate hour of your wedding (taking into account time changes) to see how many candles are needed for the desired "glow." Then check over church regulations on candles before making plans.

Lucky the bride who is wed where pews are lighted by tapers in globes. Use long strands of ivy, mint, and gray artemisias tied in place with many velvet bows to decorate the posts and create a picture perfect scene. If space permits, pedestals with Williamsburg type chimneys will support lighted candles in the aisle or chancel area.

Chancel candelabra lend themselves to similar easy ornamentation. Enhance the tall candle holders by adding bows with long streamers. Hang a wreath** in front. Tie a simple bunch of herbs on the altar boy's candle lighter.

Bridesmaids can carry lighted tapers in the manner of the Renaissance. Add bunches of herbs and bows with long streamers. The chapel needs to be breeze free for this one and perhaps the groomsmen should have extra matches available.

The passing of flame stands for unification of families and eternal joys. If the couple chooses, they might take lighted tapers and light a central wedding candle at the altar.

To make your own herbal decorated candles, press herbs from the garden for two or three days until flattened but not crisp dry. Melt down an old white candle or paraffin, brush some on to the large wedding candle, press herbs in place, then cover with another thin coat of melted wax. The wedding announcement can also be pressed into place on a good sized candle.

Check also into the use of candlelight in deep windowsills. In Spring, a fat mint-scented candle, yellow taffeta bows, and baby's breath is a simple, effective decoration. For Winter, lay down sprigs of red berried holly and red velvet bows with spicy candles. Place each arrangement on a 9" x 12" board. These make the windowsill arrangements portable, easily removed to the reception area after the service.

Love note

I have a talented friend who always likes to entertain midwinter using one hundred and fifty candles in glasses or glass chimneys throughout the house. It's a fairyland, breathtaking in the "quiet of the year."

THE RECEPTION

There are innumerable ways to include herbs in your after-the-wedding party. Whether it is held at home or at the country club or in the church hall, the bride and her mother and their informal committee of family and willing friends can add as many herbal touches as they have time for this traditional finish to the festivities. It will make all the difference.

If the party is being catered, I'm sure you can incorporate many of your ideas by consulting with the specialist in charge. He will respect your wishes for an occasion so important. If you need to rent equipment, do so early.

THE WEDDING CAKE: Ringed with snippets of fragrant herbs and colorful flowers, the cake will be in the most beautiful setting possible. Cut the herbs well in advance of the party, condition them well as instructed on page 47, and when they are crisp and perky, reduce the stems to 3" or 4" and store in a tightly covered plastic container until right before the wedding party begins. Put someone in charge of this special touch.

A charming nosegay for the top of the cake is always pretty. Arrange the herbs in oasis in a very small waterproof container painted white and place it on top of the cake. Your florist will arrange this for you too if you provide the herbs you wish included.

THE WEDDING PUNCH: The same small pieces of herbs can ring the punch bowl with or without other flowers. Remember, if you don't have access to a herb garden, this can be done with beautiful curled parsley, whole lemons and daisies — all obtainable in the market place, year round.

Top your punch with rings of ice containing lemon balm leaves, mint tips, roses, cherries or strawberries. Slices of lemon stuck with whole cloves are attractive spicy garnishes.

RECEPTION DECORATIONS: The prettiest herbal decoration is done with tall candlesticks and a gadget called an O'Bowl that holds damp oasis and sits in any regular candle holder. Charming arrangements of herbs are easily built in these candlestick containers. They can be done a day or two before the party and kept refrigerated. (Drawing page 58.)

To make a large number of centerpieces quickly, stuff the oasis with 4" pieces of durable boxwood, ivy, or evergreens early in the week before the wedding. Keep them cool and damp. Closer to party time, tuck in well conditioned herbs and a few flowers. Bows in the wedding colors are pretty too. They can made well in advance. Fifty centerpieces — if you need that many — can be made fairly quickly by a few cooperative family members, including the children. Be sure all the herbs, flowers and evergreens are cut to the same length and that they are evenly distributed in the oasis and we guarantee you the most attractive tables ever seen at a wedding. Fragrant, too.

FAVORS FOR THE WEDDING GUESTS: In certain European countries, every guest at the wedding receives a sprig of the true myrtle, symbol of love and devotion. Present it with a boutonniere pin. In others, rosemary is the treasured remembrance to be given to everyone attending. In Lithuania, where it is the national emblem, rue is distributed at weddings, as it symbolizes good luck and good health. A girl named "Melissa," of course, would wish to give out sprigs of her herb, the lemon balm.

Sweets bags of potpourri** are nice favors, fragrant and useful. Tied to a card with the names of the bride and groom along with the date will make the souvenir more meaningful. They can be made in all white bowed with the colors of the wedding party or in calico or gingham for a country wedding look.

If your theme is baskets, then little baskets or boxes** of homemade mints are a nice touch. See our recipe for the ever popular DreaMints*, hit of every party, especially when done in the wedding bell mold.

THEIR NEW HERB GARDEN

"— for now and forever"

My favorite wedding gift is a non-exchangeable door decoration, a broom corn wiskbroom tied with a bunch of fresh or dried herbs, lots of bows and a few crisp twenty dollar bills caught in the ribbons. The card to the newlyweds will read "For Mr. and Mrs. ____________'s NEW HERB GARDEN."

There is no greater joy than planning and planting, tending and harvesting a brand new little herb garden. Whether it be a few windowsill containers, a tub outside the condo door or a proper plot in a sunny spot close to their most used entrance, I always like to encourage another new herb patch. Easy to grow, the rewards are tremendous.

A small city backyard lends itself to herb gardening. Patterned paths and divided areas give a miniscule space the feel of a well planned estate. There is no doubt, that even from so small a space, herbs have the largest harvest, most pleasant and useful, of anything you can plant and tend.

Apartment herb gardening is possible in a sunny South window or, sometimes better, under growlights on the kitchen counter. Matched pots of pretty herbs can yield an unexpected amount of herbal pleasure. Keep cutting scissors handy!

If they are not gardeners, perhaps the herb garden gift money could be tied onto a good basic how-to-grow-and-use-them type herbal.

As in days of old, the gardens that supplied the wedding herbs can be counted upon to provide some starts for the newest herb garden. In turn, when the couple moves on to their second home they can take along small plants. A few herbs (plants, seeds or divisions) are treasured moments of their honeymoon haven, easily transferred to another garden plot.

Brave brides once carried such precious cargo in saddle bags or covered wagons. It is time honored tradition dating back to the Mayflower when packets of herb seeds were brought to new homes to be nurtured, treasured and used through the years.

A little garden in which to walk, an immensity in which to dream, at one's feet that which can be cultivated and plucked; overhead that which one can study and meditate upon; some herbs on earth and all the stars in the sky.

— Hugo

AROMATHERAPY

or "Please Pass the Smelling Salts!"

I'm convinced we make so much ado about weddings because of the importance of such an event in one's life. It ranks with birth and death, over which one has little control. The emotional build-up equals or exceeds the wear and tear on the nerves. This nervous energy in turn fuels the wedding preparation activity which mounts with the proximity to the date. Nerves and stress become synonymous — a truism that has always been so. Herbs to the rescue!

To counteract the stress of expanding wedding preparations, and indeed the wedding day itself, surround yourself and everyone involved with fragrances. Now called "Aromatherapy," herbs have been found to work well to relieve nerves and stress. Books have been written on the subject of "Aromatherapy" and great universities have researched the effectiveness of fragrance and herbs. Their calming influence cannot be denied.

Try it for yourself. Herbs can quiet the nerves and temper emotions as needed. Breathe deeply and enjoy fragrances that please you. Drink herbal teas while engaged in the seemingly endless wedding projects and preparations. And treat yourself to many relaxing herbal baths. They work wonders.

Love note *THE BRIDE WAS SCENT-SATIONAL! You've planned this wedding for months. Do schedule a few relaxing hours for the most important person — the bride — and her personal needs. Enjoy a soothing bath with a favorite bath oil, thinking only beautiful unhurried thoughts. Wrap yourself in a big fluffy towel and then begin "layering your fragrance" for a long and lasting aura. Use body lotions, followed by the sweet caress of perfumed talc. Spray cologne on your hair for a "veil of scent" and, while you are at it, scent an heirloom hanky to tuck in your sleeve. Saturate cottonballs with your favorite scent and stich them on the hem of your petticoat and know that you walk in beauty all during your unforgettable day.*

HERBS FOR THE BATH

1 c. mint
1 c. rosemary
1 c. lavender flowers
1 c. rosepetals
1 c. comfrey leaves
1 c. lovage

Combine the dried herbs and store in a clear glass jar. They are decorative as well as useful. Simmer a cupful in 1 qt. water for 5 minutes. Strain into your bath water and relax. Think only about what you have already crossed off your list of things to be done.

HERBS SAY THE NICEST THINGS FOR ANNIVERSARIES

Let's not overlook anniversaries. The years pile up. Before you know it, another anniversary is here.

Once again, the herbal ideas for menus, punch bowls, gifts, favors and decorations abound. There are traditional anniversary symbols as well as a few more recent tokens to consider. Select your theme and color scheme from this accepted list and start planning the party. Use ideas from THE BRIDE'S HERBAL and see for yourself the many ways that "Herbs Make the Difference." From *paper* to *diamonds*, the lavish use of herbs lend themselves to all celebrations. Their enchantment will linger long after the party ends, until the next anniversary.

A husband is the only labor-saving device you can cuddle.

WEDDING ANNIVERSARIES

Year	Traditional	Modern
First	Paper	Wine/Flowers
Second	Cotton	Books
Third	Leather	House Plants
Fourth	Flowers	Pottery
Fifth	Wood	Crystal/Glass
Sixth	Candy	Copper
Seventh	Wool	Linens
Eighth	Bronze	Wood
Ninth	Pottery	Pewter
Tenth	Tin	Art
Eleventh	Steel	Gourmet Cookware
Twelfth	Silk	Leather
Thirteenth	Lace	Clocks/Watches
Fourteenth	Ivory	Iron
Fifteenth	Crystal	Pearls
Twentieth	China	China
Twenty-fifth	Silver	Silver
Thirtieth	Pearl	Coral
Thirty-fifth	Coral	Jade
Fortieth	Ruby	Ruby
Forty-fifth	Sapphire	Sapphire
Fiftieth	Gold	Gold
Fifty-fifth	Emerald	Emerald
Sixtieth	Diamond	Diamond
Seventy-fifth	Diamond	Diamond

WEDDING FLOWERS

IDEAS FOR THE BRIDAL BOUQUET

The eloquence of herbs is never more apparent than in a bridal bouquet. They speak of many things — of ancient wisdom and future joy.

The three most important wedding herbs are myrtle, orange blossom, and rosemary, of course. They were used for centuries to decorate wedding halls, as garlands, crowns, and bridal bouquets.

The Romans crowned their brides with myrtle, a delightfully fragrant small-leaved evergreen shrub. True *Myrtus communis* is not the creeping ground cover we call myrtle today. Emblem of "divine generosity," sprigs of true myrtle are still worn traditionally by bride or groom in many European countries, a carry over from those Roman days. The maid-of-honor took home a sprig of the bridal crown of myrtle which she was expected to root as a symbol of her own future love and happiness, perhaps to be worn in her wedding crown.

Throughout the eastern civilization far back in antiquity, the true myrtle is revered as a symbol of wedded bliss. The Egyptians, Hebrews, Romans, and ancient Greeks have recorded the virtues of this fragant, almost sacred, herb and always in association with love and marriage.

Orange blossoms are still coveted by today's bride with traditional leanings. The waxen white blossoms with overpowering fragrance are symbolic of joy and happiness and fecundity. Scent and sentiment abound for brides wearing orange blossoms. Because they are sometimes hard to get, the equally fragrant white blossoms of the Ponderosa lemon tree, a houseplant, make a good substitute.

Rosemary speaks also of joy and good wishes in a bridal bouquet. Shakespeare referred to the charming wedding party custom of distributing sprigs of gilded rosemary tied with ribbons called "bride's laces."

Because it is symbolic of love and loyalty, bridesmaids once long ago presented the bridegroom with a bunch of rosemary on his wedding morning. A sprig of rosemary was always included in the bride's bouquet — this was to insure happiness and good luck.

We have perhaps overlooked these "loving herbs" because they are greenhouse plants in northern climates and not always easy to find. "Second day air" may make it possible today (see sources). All may be grown as houseplants, summered outdoors. Indeed they are quite satisfactory as potplants if supplied with a sunny window, cool room, good soil and some humidity. However, dried myrtle leaves, rosemary, as well as orange blossom oil is always available.

HERBAL WEDDING BOUQUETS

A simple bunch of herbs and flowers can be carried as is or placed into a circular bouquet (a tussie-mussie) or arranged in a basket for an informal wedding.

It is most important to know that all herbs should be well conditioned before arranging, especially in spring. Cut them a day before and place them promptly in warm water (not submerged). If possible, a floral conditioner and refrigeration will also help prevent wilting. Remember, too, your herbs are important to the ambience and meaning of your wedding. We don't want them wilting during the few hours they are in use. Be sure herbs from the garden, especially in spring and summer, are extemely well conditioned. Because they grow so fast, they wilt easily once cut.

If you wish, you can find a cooperative florist who will work the herbs into the wedding flowers for you. See to it that he has them in plenty of time before the wedding so he knows what he is doing.

HERB BOUQUET ON A HOOP: This is pretty and easy to do. Purchase a 14" wooden hoop from a craft shop with macrame supplies, wrap it with white satin ribbon, beginning and ending with Scotch tape. Where you use the tape, affix an informal bouquet of herbs with or without other flowers, tie it on securely. It may need to be tied twice so that it doesn't slip. The bride and her bridesmaids can carry it over the rim, in front, with herbs at the top or the bottom of the hoop. Ribbon streamers are also optional. The nice part about these bouquets is that they can be used during the reception as decorations. Determine in advance a place to hang them effectively.

HERBAL TUSSIE-MUSSIE: A more formal kind of bouquet, these circular nosegays are popular for proms, anniversaries and many occasions as well as for brides. Starting with a central flower, place short stemmed herbs around it in concentric circles of greens, grays, blue-greens and so on. Continue with rounds of flowers, preferably fragrant, and herbs until it is a nice size to carry.

White or colored flowers can be used. One or more different kinds of herbs may be included. It can be all rosemary if you like or a mixture of herbs chosen for their symbolism or their availability.

Net, bows, streamers, lace and doilies are all optional. It can be all white or assorted colors, as you like. Cover stems with foil or, more elegant, florist tape covered with velvet ribbon secured with straight pins.

Sometimes the bride provides the herbs, takes them to her local florist and he will arrange them, along with other flowers, into a nosegay.

BASKET OF HERBS: Choose a basket with which you are comfortable. Carry it about and see if it fits. Line it with plastic then stuff with well saturated oasis (available at any florist). Then, using short stems of well conditioned herbs, fill the basket. Poke in the herbs, using the one you have the most of first and filling in with the others as you go along. Flowers may be included, of course, and bows are always pretty. In making such a basket, work with stems of the same length and remember that there's always room for "just one more."

Sometimes a small bunch of the herbs is tucked in the center, to be removed and thrown at the end of the reception party. Be sure the herbs are well secured if you think the bride will toss them vigorously.

Take thou this rose, O rose
Since love's own flower it is,
And by that rose
That lover captive is.

Anonymous Renaissance Troubadour

LITTLE NOSEGAYS: One of our loveliest herbal weddings was done for an older woman who wanted to share her joy with many family members. (See page 32, "The Second Wedding.")

PRAYER BOOK HERBS: Gather about two dozen sprigs of herbs. Divide them into two groups and cover their stems with florist tape. Placing one bunch up and the other down, tie them together in the middle using narrow white satin bridal ribbons with streamers. Keep this herbal delight in plastic under refrigeration until you are ready to attach it to your Prayer Book. If it is a family heirloom, have a picture taken and paste it inside the book for posterity.

WEDDING MATS: These are gay and unusual — attendant's will love them. Using a flat wicker mat, weave ribbons through the outer openings leaving streamers at the bottom and attaching a pipe cleaner handle to the back. Prayer Book Herbs (above) can be attached to the center of the mats carried by all the attendants. Tuck in some dried rosebuds along with other pods and herbs that dry well such as yarrow, knotted marjoram, lunaria "silver dollars," lavender, or baby's breath and it will become a gift-decoration the bridesmaid can hang on her wall after the wedding is over.

That love is all there is
Is all we know of love.
— Emily Dickinson

BOUTONNIERES

A sprig of rosemary with a fluffy white carnation is always acceptable. Of course it could match the bride's bouquet with a rose or daisy or other flower.

A tiny bunch of herbs with a touch of lace and baby's breath is a simple timely boutonniere.

POCKET POSIES — Instead of conventional boutonnieres, consider "pocket posies," a handful of fragrant symbolic herbs gathered into a small bunch. If I am wearing a jacket with a breast pocket, I always stuff it with a casual bunch of herbs . . . mint, lavender, santolina, southernwood, scented geraniums, whatever. Patted as the day progresses, it perfumes the air, alerts the senses as nothing else can, and constitutes "aromatherapy." Dare to be different! A generous handful of herbs for each groomsman, gathered in advance and kept fresh under refrigeration is a wonderful added touch. Useful too when little things go wrong — and they always do. Just pat the fragrant pocket posies, breathe deeply, and relax.

THE HERBAL HEART BOUQUET

A heart shaped herb bouquet is timeless, perfect for both bride and bridesmaid; the girl whose engagement is being announced; or in miniature for the junior attendant or flower girl.

The "heart outline" bouquet is easy to create. Here is a simple method of construction. Wrap two #20 gauge wires with white or colored floratape stemwrap and bend the first wire to form the outline of slightly more than one-half a heart, depending on the size you wish your finished heart to be. You may find it easier to cut a paper heart and use that as the pattern from which the wire outline is made (Fig. 1). For a sturdier frame use a heart-shaped coat hanger or two pieces of wire can be intertwined as shown in the sketch. The outline is finished by adding the second tape covered wire and joining the two using spiral twist (Fig. 2).

Select short snippets of herbs and flower buds. Add each bud to the frame and overwrap with stem wrap in the chosen color. Sweetheart roses, hyacinth florets, stephanotis, feathered carnations are some of the flowers to combine with herbs. Add the flowers on the

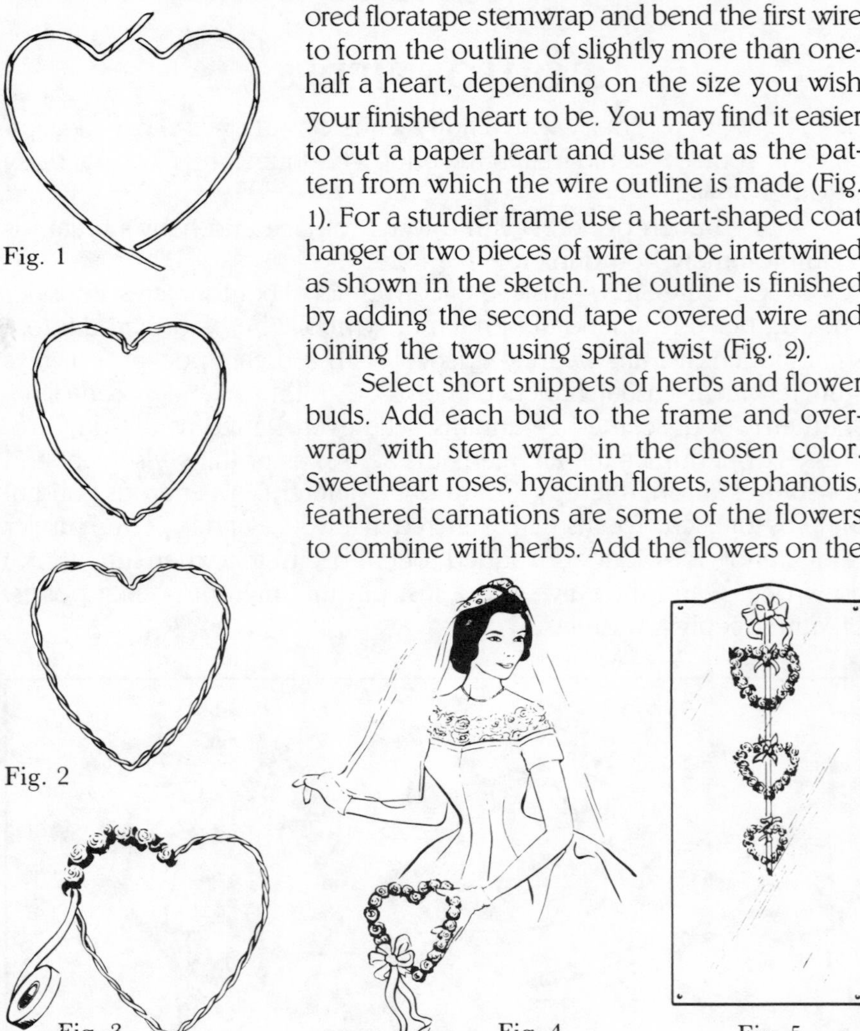

Fig. 1

Fig. 2

Fig. 3

Fig. 4

Fig. 5

front face of the heart, taping them in place in succession. Work from the top center down on one side and then on the other, always covering the stems with the heads of each succeeding herb and flower (Fig. 3).

To give a graceful finish to the bouquet we suggest adding a velvet ribbon and herbal accent just off center near the base. A bouquet of this style is held in the hand at the top or side. No handles are required Fig. 4).

Several herbal hearts may be tied together with a series of ribbons and used on a mirror or front door for an engagement announcement or anniversary (Fig. 5). Made in miniature with a lighter gauge wire, they make an unusual and sentimental corsage to be worn by the person with a flair for the unusual. Dare to use little herbal hearts as boutonnieres too.

HERBAL CHAPLETS

With or without veiling, a crown of precious herbs and small flowers is an enchanting hairpiece. As they have since ancient Roman times, the bride (or her bridesmaids) will be blessed with the wearing. Little girls and big are prettier wearing fragrant herbs and flowers in their hair or on a wide-brimmed hat.

Making such a charmed circle is not difficult. A day or two before the wedding, gather your herbs and small flowers — rosebuds, clove pinks, lily-of-the-valley, violets, daisies, small zinnias, lilacs, mums and many others. Condition them well in warm water for several hours. Do not submerge. When the herbs and flowers are filled with as much moisture as possible, you can start working. Several willing friends would be a great help if there are many halos to be made.

You will need:

- a thin wire coathanger
- white florist tape
- 3 yds. narrow satin ribbon (or more)
- white nylon tulle (optional)
- baby's breath (optional)

1. Form a wire ring from the coathanger to fit the crown of the head and cover it with the white florist tape. When working with florist tape, stretch and pull it, smoothing it around the wire. This should be done well in advance.

2. Cut all herbs and flowers into 2"-3" pieces.
3. Cut a few 3" pieces of ribbon and a few 4" squares of the net.
4. Place a herb or two against the wire and wrap with florist tape.
5. Without cutting the tape, lay another snippet or two of herbs and flowers overlapping the first one and taping securely.
6. Continue on at this pace, always overlapping the herbs and using a continuous piece of tape, occasionally including a loop of ribbon and tuft of the net until the hairpiece is well covered, balanced, and completed. Tuck in baby's breath, too, if you wish.
7. Complete your hairpiece with the ribbons, attaching it in little bows here and there or one bow with streamers at the back.
8. Attach hair combs in several places.
9. Spray very lightly with water then keep the herbal hairpiece in a plastic bag under refrigeration until needed. It will keep well for a day or two.

VEILS: Ancient Roman brides carried bunches of herbs under their wedding veils. Later, the Saracens carried orange blossoms as a symbol of fertility. An Austrian custom is to cross the veil with a wreath of fresh myrtle, ancient flower of love. A chaplet of herbs is easier used as a circlet to anchor the veiling. Bridal veils may also be attached to the back of a traditional halo.

HAIR COMBS with herbs and bows attached are another easy hairpiece, becoming to every member of the wedding. Keep fresh herbs on combs wrapped in plastic under refrigeration until the last possible moment.

If all this seems too much to handle that close to the wedding, take your herbs to your nearest friendly florist and he will make your chaplet for you.

Thou silver glow worm, oh lend me they light,
I must gather the mystic St. John'swort tonight;
The wonderful herb, whose leaf will decide
If the coming year shall make me a bride.

(Pluck your St. John'swort on the eve of St. John, June 24, Midsummer's Night. The longer the flowers and leaves last, the better the chance of marriage within the year — or so they say.)

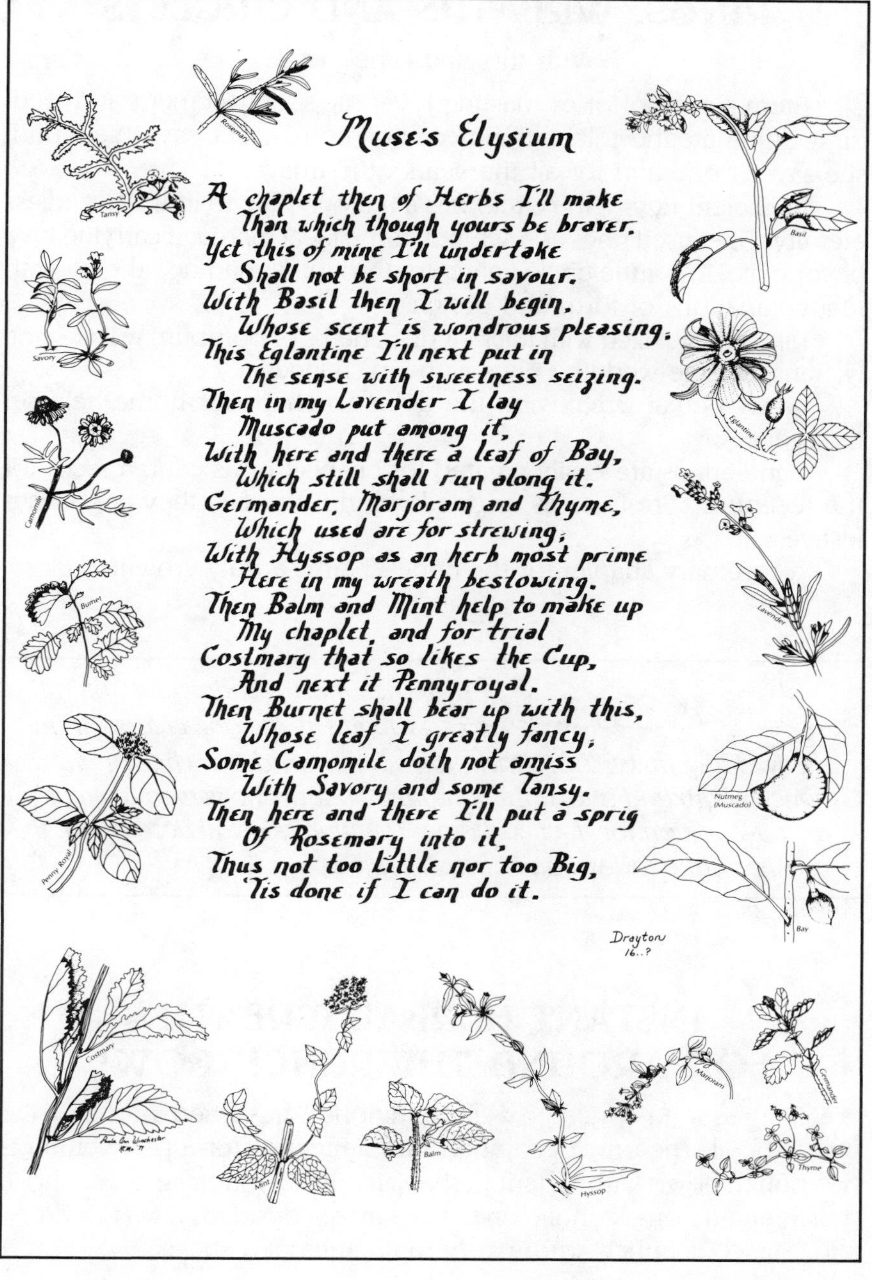

Muse's Elysium

A chaplet then of Herbs I'll make
  Than which though yours be braver,
Yet this of mine I'll undertake
  Shall not be short in savour.
With Basil then I will begin,
  Whose scent is wondrous pleasing.
This Eglantine I'll next put in
  The sense with sweetness seizing.
Then in my Lavender I lay
  Muscado put among it,
With here and there a leaf of Bay,
  Which still shall run along it.
Germander, Marjoram and Thyme,
  Which used are for strewing;
With Hyssop as an herb most prime
  Here in my wreath bestowing.
Then Balm and Mint help to make up
  My chaplet, and for trial
Costmary that so likes the Cup,
  And next it Pennyroyal.
Then Burnet shall bear up with this,
  Whose leaf I greatly fancy,
Some Camomile doth not amiss
  With Savory and some Tansy.
Then here and there I'll put a sprig
  Of Rosemary into it,
Thus not too Little nor too Big,
  'Tis done if I can do it.

Drayton
16..?

RINGS, WREATHS AND CIRCLETS

"With this ring I thee wed"

Eternal symbol of everlasting love, rings, engagement and wedding, dominate the celebration from the moment she says "Yes" until she says "I do" and for all the years of marriage.

In ancient Egypt, the circle was a hieroglyphic to indicate endless eternity. They used rings as a symbol of the ideal marriage carrying love beyond life. This little circle can carry through a marriage theme with many variations of form and design.

Ring pillows filled with fragrant dried herbs or potpourri will elegantly transport the wedding rings to be exchanged.

Pretty herbal wreaths on the doors to chapel or home help set the scene.

Candlerings are easily created for chancel or as centerpieces for the reception. Fresh herbs or dried colorful flowers, they are always festive.

A rosemary chaplet for the bride's hair is a truly crowning glory.

Love note *The most sentimental of all wreaths is the one created from the wedding flowers. Dry them (or have them dried while on your honeymoon) and attach the romantic bouquet flowers to a wreath as a decoration for the new home. The ultimate wall decoration, it is a keepsake to love and cherish forever.*

INSTANT HERBAL WREATH FOR AROUND THE PUNCH BOWL

Lay assorted sprigs of well conditioned fresh herbs around the punch bowl. The only decoration more effective for a party buffet is two punch bowls with instant herbal wreaths. If you have an alcoholic punch and a non-alcoholic one, it is a most considerate way to entertain. Stir your punch with a very long cinnamon stick.

To assemble your instant fresh herb wreath, cut 4" to 6" pieces of bright green curled parsley, grayed oregano, soft lamb's ear, both green and gray santolina, pale marjoram, aromatic Sweet Annie, all the basils, ferny southernwood, chartreuse lemon balm, mints of all kinds, rosemary in abundance and scented geraniums. Clip a goodly assortment, toss them in warm water in your sink to freshen them, condition them in a dishpanful of water to which a floral preservative has been added, drain them, pop the whole shebang into a large plastic bag and keep it under refrigeration until needed. Scatter them around the bowls or cake plate. Thus prepared, your fresh herbs will last through a long party without water.

STREWING HERBS: A CENTERPIECE

In Biblical times in the Temples and during Medieval times in dark monasteries and drafty castles, herbs were used to strew on the floors where the fragrant greens were expected to keep away creepie-crawlies, dispel the pestilence in the air and make gatherings fragrant for people. So be it today — but with a difference.

Strew rose petals and little snippets of herbs along the path of the bride, just a few will do, as a symbolic gesture.

STREWING HERB CENTERPIECES: Here's an easy way to decorate, using well conditioned snippets of herbs. Cut and condition enough for the number of tables at your reception. Keep them in a large plastic bag under refrigeration (a spare refrigerator is good for this purpose) until needed. Mobilize your committee of friendly neighbors and helpful family to "strew the herbs." Tell them

1. where they are kept under refrigeration
2. what time to do it — while the official photos are being taken and before the guests arrive at the party
3. how to "strew the herbs" (anyone can do it)

If your tables are round, use a circular motif. If they are long, they can be strewn in a serpentine effect down the center.

First lay down a "roadway" of lacy white paper doilies. Instead of the doilies you could substitute flat leather leaf fern from the florist (which is already conditioned) or flat lacy Arbor vitae pieces, 4-6" long, from the nearest hedge. These will need to be conditioned by tossing them in a laundry tub of warm sugar water (a cupful of sugar to a gallon of water). Allow them to remain overnight before draining the water then store the greens in a plastic bag in a cool place for later use.

At the appointed time, the short snippets of fragrant herbs and colorful garden flowers or roses of your choice can be laid in place along the "roadway." Strew them along the front of the head table, as thickly or as thinly as your supply of herbs allows.

To ornament your centerpieces, include some little flowers, daisies, roses, or whatever is compatible with your wedding theme. Here is where you tuck in paper fans, butterflies, or favorite things, white wedding balls, little baskets of mints, or use just bows, all white or bows matching the wedding party's color harmony.

Candlesticks may be added if you like, identical ones if you have enough, assorted sized ones that are all silver or glass, or low vigil lights in colorful glass containers are fanciful. Their glow resembles stained glass when lit.

Include small stand-up cards,** handwritten, explaining the symbolism of the herbs in your "strewing herb centerpiece." All your guests will enjoy reading and knowing about the ancient plants you are using in your wedding theme.

EASY CENTERPIECES

For those who are already skilled flower arrangers, no instructions are necessary. For others, I encourage you to use herbs and flowers en masse in huge full branches, or a single stem can be outstanding. Practice a bit, enjoy the challenge and don't be intimidated.

GROUPINGS OF ASSORTED SIZED CANDLES and candlesticks are always effective. Incorporate a few scented candles too. Very simple, bedded on cut herbs and greens, a few flowers in florist picks of water will add that finishing touch. Place each grouping on a board or base for easy placement and removal.

MUSHROOM BASKETS available from your family greengrocer make practical centerpieces. Tie each midway with pretty lace or ribbons and fill the baskets with 3" pots of herbs, labeled. Perhaps you will do this well in advance so line the basket with plastic and foil for carefree watering. Tuck in some excelsior or Spanish moss at the last minute. Add bows.

STARK WHITE is ideal for any wedding occasion, especially a bridal brunch. Collect white milkglass budvases of all sizes and shapes. I went to a local flea market and bought six, each different, in one hour. Fill them with single stems of herbs and assorted flowers, one of each to a vase. Arrange in groups down long tables or center several on round tables. This is charming and informal enough for any wedding herbfest.

TUSSIE-MUSSIE CENTERPIECES. Gather all the herbs you can get and group them into many bunches. Condition the small bunches in a shallow pan of warm water in the refrigerator for several hours or overnight. Damp paper towels or wet moss (a Victorian contrivance) wrapped around the stems then protected by plastic or foil will keep them from wilting. Ribbons and lace collars are elegant finishing touches. These make wonderful centerpieces. Attach them to tall supports (supported dowels or very tall wine bottles will work) with ribbons dangling midair. Groupings of these topiary-like bouquets are even more effective than one by one. Or lay one atop napkin covered boxes or flower pots that serve as pedestals to elevate them. NOTE: Let me give you a tip. Recycle any stray fragments of beauty or fragrance you can in these happy little bunches. It lends greater charm than you can imagine. And please don't lament a seeming lack of professional craftsmanship! Not at all essential, that is why they are so endearing.

FOR A MORE ELEGANT EFFECT, suitable for after four affairs, collect assorted silver and glass antique budvases then arrange them on mirrors along with low vigil lights. Plain white warmer candles in clear glass tumblers add sparkle to the ambiance. It's fun, too, to give each lady guest a budvase to take along home, token of your herbal wedding.

If time permits and you are so inclined, prepare bows (in advance) with little white tags bearing the name and symbolism for each sprig of herb. It is guaranteed conversation at the party.

TABLE TOO NARROW FOR CENTERPIECES? Use wine glasses holding tiny herbal nosegays at each place.

SOFT SCULPTURE POTS OF HERBS become entertaining centerpieces or favors (or both). Cover the pots with plastic or foil so they may be watered easily and kept alive. Wrap the ordinary pots with batting or tissue. Tie a calico square of suitable size around the rim with contrasting ribbons or wool to tie it in place.

OASIS (Reg.) has devised many useful forms of water absorbing floral foam for wreaths, blocks, posey holders, stick-ons for doors, walls and mirrors, candlestick o'dapters, pew bow bouquet holders and more.

Your local craft shop or florist can assist you in finding these undeniably useful tools, all of which lend themselves to herbal wedding work. They are designed to make floral designs of all kinds ridiculously easy. Compact and versatile, just soak the oasis; once filled with water, start inserting the short well conditioned sprigs of herbs and flowers.

CREATIVE IDEAS FOR THE HERBAL WEDDING

IF YOU WRITE YOUR OWN CEREMONY, or any part of it, touch it with the quiet dignity of the symbolism of your wedding herbs.

IT IS ALSO WISE TO PRINT THE LIST OF HERBS AND THEIR SYMBOLISM in the church wedding program if you are having one. You'll discover that most people will save unusual programs such as these, enjoying the sentiment expressed in your choice of herbs. It's also a grand opportunity for the happy couple to extend a verbal "tussie-mussie" of accolades to all who helped with the herbs, a time to express their joy and gratitude. (See Index for symbolism.) You can incorporate the same herbal meanings in anniversary celebrations, of course.

THE RING BEARER'S PILLOW stuffed with fragrant dried herbs — or potpourri — becomes a "scentimental" keepsake to enjoy forever for pillow talk or between your linens. Personalize it with your monogram and the date or use our beautiful "Rosemary for Remembrance" sampler.*** If, after a while, the pillow seems to lose its fragrance, renew it with a few drops of your favorite essential oil.

DESIGN YOUR OWN INVITATIONS OR ANNOUNCEMENTS incorporating your "favorite things" theme, chosen color harmony and a sprig of pressed herbs. Hand written, they can easily be printed on good card stock. Take them to your neighborhood printer and he will advise you.

PRETTY HANDWRITING makes the most attractive and charming labels. Herbs assume their proper role when people know what they are and why you chose to use them. Let them express the traditional bridal wishes for health, love and prosperity. If you don't have the most decorative hand, perhaps a friend will write your message or you can employ a calligrapher. Dress it with your "favorite things" theme and have it printed in your chosen color harmony by your friendly printer.

AS GUESTS ENTER THE CHURCH, revive the old world custom of giving each of them a sprig of herbs — for instance lavender for the bride's family and friends, rosemary for the groom's side. A little boutonniere pin might be handy. Tell the ushers about this charming tradition and which herb is which so they are knowledgeable.

TODAY'S BRIDAL BOUQUETS have changed. You may carry a single long-stemmed rose with a sprig of rosemary if you so desire. In this case "less is more" and most impressive.

THE MOTHER'S CORSAGES are sometimes better worn on a clutch bag or as a wristlet. If such is the case, fragrant herbs in or on the hands are heavenly to waft about on a hot summer's day.

SHEAVES OF WHEAT are a symbolic gesture dating back to the Renaissance. Use them, with herbs, in lieu of bouquets or as decorations throughout the house, on the doors of home or church, and at the reception. It is particularly effective for a Fall wedding.

FLOAT FLOWERS AND HERBS on squares of styrofoam in a garden pool for an outdoor summer wedding. They will float free, peacefully and beautifully, delighting the senses.

TIE A SMALL BUNCH OF HERBS ON THE CAKE KNIFE. Traditional lily-of-the-valley, in silk if it is out of season, can be included. Tie it with the usual narrow white ribbon streamers.

AT THE SHOWER, have handy several yards of narrow white ribbon, a large flat wicker mat and a bowl of freshly picked mint or assorted herbs. As the packages are unwrapped, affix all bows to the wicker mat using the white ribbon. Tuck a little bunch of herbs (4 or 6 sprigs) into the center of each bow and tie securely. When the party is over and you are finished, your guest of honor will have a colorful fragrant door decoration for their new apartment. The herbs will dry in place and

and she can keep it as long as she likes. It could be packed away for the tenth anniversary party!

INFORM YOUR PHOTOGRAPHER to be sure to include herbal vignettes in his pictures to enhance your album of memories of this special day. Press some of the herbs to glue between the pictures ornamenting your treasured keepsake. It sets the scene by reinforcing your theme.

RAISING THE ROOF — For a different bridal shower conversation piece, build a miniature house of heavy cardboard, a large box will work, constructed so that the peaked roof lifts off. Paint it white, with windows of colored paper pasted in place. On the side, print the honored couples' names and date in large letters. Surround the house with bunches of fragrant herbs such as mint, lemon balm, artemisias, costmary, angelica and so forth. Fill the little house with wrapped gifts for the home.

ROSES FOR LOVE — In England, they toss fresh rose petals at the happy couple. If June is your wedding month and the rose garden is in full bloom, have a friend gather fully open roses the night before, pull the petals off and pop them into a plastic bag, then into the refrigerator. Add to your reminder list for the day — "Fill baskets (at the ready) with refrigerated rose petals and give to appointed young relatives to distribute to wedding guests assembled outside the church." NOTE: These are bio-degradable. They curl up and disappear all on their own within a few hours of the wedding. No need to sweep the sidewalk.

A FRESH TUSSIE-MUSSIE FOR THE DECEMBER BRIDE? — Yes! You can gather certain hardy herb tips even in severe climates — thyme, winter savory, sage, rue, lavender, southernwood, burnet, hyssop — toss them in a bucket of warm water saying "Wake up!" And they will spring back to life. Combine with rosemary and myrtle from the windowsill and a few florist flowers, say "roses for love," to make a traditional circular nosegay. Laces and ribbons may be added.

LOVE BATH BALLS are fun, perfect Valentine or bridal tokens, both fragrant and scentimental. They can be tucked into ivy nosegays for color and aroma or just as easily mailed out as invitations along with your message of love. The ingredients are readily available either from your garden, on your pantry shelves or from your nearest herb shop. See my recipe *Herbs for the Bath* on page 42 which will make a dozen or more darling little bath balls. Don't mislay anything this versatile!

In fact, this recipe might also double as a Valentine tea or as sachets.

DON'T OVERLOOK THE VEGETABLE GARDEN — Beautiful centerpieces can be created using vegetables, especially if you have a garden from which they may be gathered. Pick and polish whatever you have available. Have you ever studied a cabbage? It is a big beautiful rose. Arrange a grouping of cabbages, partially opened, on a flat white wicker basket. Fill in with bunches of parsley, red basil, watercress or your biggest heads of fragrant dill. Cover your table with a green and white patterned fabric and use napkins of hot pink. Roll them into a scroll, tie with ribbon and tuck in a sprig of rosemary. Stunning!

EGGPLANT CAN BE DRAMATIC! Peppers, red and green and yellow, are jewels! If you don't grow your own, look over the display in your favorite market then buy a great quantity of everything in season. Use them as decor all through the house as well as an edible centerpiece in the Williamsburg manner.

SPECIAL TABLECLOTHS — A popular hobby today is hand-painting of fabrics. It's easy and fun to do. Enjoy and display your creativity by decorating it for a special bridal party. Using a white background, purchased or stitched to fit the tables, design your cloths with "favorite things" in the color theme or use fabric pens in hot pinks, reds, soft greens and lavenders, yellows, orange and heavenly blues. Be sure to embroider with your pen all the herbs your party will include. Write out the symbolism. Such a memorable keepsake will be treasured by the bride if you decide to give it to her as a gift. Simple squares are easiest to do. Use undercloths with them and napkins to match the table skirts. Perhaps your guests would like to sign their names. (Dover Books has a HERB COLORING BOOK with simple large drawings of many herbs.)

SPICE FAVORS — In Austria, there is a little shop that sells "spice posies" to fragrance the kitchen. Bits of whole cloves, cinnamon, allspice, ginger and nutmeg are glued onto a lacy white paper doily to be hung over the stove where the steamy heat of cooking releases the spicy fragrance. It could, of course, be kept under a glass dome in the living room, opened to sniff, closed to keep it pretty and fragrant and clean. Spices, dried golden yarrow, glue, doilies, and ribbons are all you need to make these delightful old-world charmers. It's easy to glue the whole spices into the golden heads of yarrow, an herb for "a love that lasts." Use them as the centerpiece, later to be distributed as favors.

MORE CREATIVE IDEAS FOR HERBAL WEDDINGS

TO MAKE GOOD USE OF TIME AND SCHEDULING, cut attractive small patterned evergreens such as boxwood, juniper, Korean holly, azalea, and so forth, to use as a basis for many last minute fresh herb bouquets and decorations. Secure the heavy stemmed evergreens in wet Oasis covered and reinforced with chicken wire (if necessary). Keep the bases cool and misted for up to two weeks before the party or wedding. At the last minute, well conditioned sage, rosemary, lavender, rue and southernwood are quickly and easily added along with any colorful flowers you have. Bows, finished weeks ahead, complete the projects.

PREI DIEU — If your church uses a kneeling bench, devise a simple rectangular herbal sachet for your wedding. Embroider it with initials and the date. As you kneel on the fragrant pillow, glorious aromas will be released into the air. Afterwards the flat pillow will serve as yet another keepsake, a sachet for your linen closet.

HAVE YOUR HERBAL BRIDAL BOUQUET PHOTOGRAPHED PROFESSIONALLY close up. Then, as they did in Victorian days, commission an artist to paint it on canvas, framed for posterity. Insert small prints of the photograph in your "thank you" notes for one last romantic souvenir.

ALTAR AND CHANCEL HERBAL BOUQUETS can do double duty as centerpieces at the reception. Put the ushers in charge of transporting the church bouquets after the official photographs are taken.

If she's from Long Island and he's from San Diego, assist your guests in finding housing and entertainment before and after the ceremony. Your special day could prove to be a long weekend. Fragrant bunches of herbs should welcome them in their rooms upon arrival along with a greeting on herbal notepaper listing the schedule of events, things to do in the area, perhaps an invitation to a brunch buffet on Saturday or Sunday, special places to visit (local herb gardens), and useful phone numbers. This is a good area to enlist the aid of willing friends and other family members living in the area. Remember memories are made by extra little herbal touches.

PEW BOWS take kindly to herbs. Use them to mark seating for V.I.P.'s or more lavishly by placing one at every other pew all along the main aisle for a truly dramatic setting.

In spring or summer, hang the herb bunches upside down, as if to dry, so they can wilt gracefully. In fall, when weather has conditioned them, arrange casual handsfull of herbs upright in each bow.

The Oasis people have come out with a nifty gadget designed especially for pew bows. Supporting a round piece of floral foam that can be used wet or dry, the bows, herbs and flowers are quickly poked into place. Then simply hang the entire arrangement over the edge of the pew by an attached hook. There is absolutely no fiddling with wires, ribbons or masking tape. The Rosemary House has the pew holders or perhaps your local florist can get them for you. The Oasis is replaceable and they are reusable.

MY IDEA OF HEAVEN would be to be wed in one of the thousand acre mint farms in our mid-west or Oregon . . . while it's being harvested. Oh, joy!

SEASHELLS ARE A VERSATILE COLLECTIBLE. A great motif that ties in nicely with herbs, get out your old collection. Pile them down the center of tables with herbs and flowers here and there and sand surrounding all. Add little candles too. Colored glasses holding warmer candles sparkle like stained glass. Use the seashells as butter pats, for individual dips, as sauce dishes, as tea bag holders, while larger ones are wonderful salad plates, especially to serve seafood. Stuffed with sprigs of herbs, they become both centerpieces and favors. Piled high with potpourri is another way to set the scene with seashells.

LARGE POTS OF WELL GROWN ROSEMARIES or other herbs can be recycled from the patio party, to showers, to line the steps into the church, to the reception, and eventually to the honeymoon cottage garden. Rosemary topiaries are particularly outstanding decorations. Plans for topiaries and herbs in large pots require working at least a year in advance.

HAVE THE FLOWER GIRLS CARRY BASKETS of fragrant potpourri, made well in advance, to strew (if allowed) or not, as you wish.

DECORATE THE RICE BASKET and the flower girls' baskets with bunches of herbs, fresh or dried, and ribbons of the wedding colors.

BE SURE TO PLACE A BOUQUET OF FRAGRANT HERBS and flowers by the guest book. Tie a sprig of rosemary on the pen.

A "SOFT" FRAME with satin, laces and ribbons can be easily scented with a drop or two of essential oil.

MORE FAVORS — Plastic bathroom tiles heated in a 280 deg. oven until soft and pliable can be shaped over something with a flat bottom for little herb bouquets or to hold a bit of potpourri or as individual mint dishes. They look like ceramic and make lovely little favors.

FRUIT FAVORS — As individual favors, core a green pear or red apple and fill with a bunch of parsley, herbs and tiny flowers. One for each guest will harvest you rave reviews.

MORE HERBAL WEDDING CRAFTS

HERBAL WREATHS

HERB WREATHS are the loveliest of all decorations. If you want to set the scene with this joyous welcome, they can be made up to a year in advance and used many times over, throughout the pre-nuptial proceedings and for the wedding itself. Cut the herbs from your garden when available and you will have the wreaths when you need them.

HOW TO MAKE HERBAL WREATHS

When the herb garden comes into its seasonal harvest, it yields the greatest pleasure. Time to make herb wreaths. There is no pleasanter task with greater rewards. Use them as fragrant decorations for your home, flat on the tables, on the church doors, and everywhere you would want an attractive unusual herbal touch. They can be made well in advance of the event and they make the best possible "thank you" gifts for helpful family, friends, neighbors and members of the wedding party.

If you have only a mint patch, you can make a lovely fragrant wreath or two. If your garden also contains lemon balm, sage, southernwood, tansy or any of the silvery artemisias, you are in business. Cut a large basket full of snippets, the cuttings need be only 6" long, and fill your house with fragrance while you work on this project.

If you need additional material to eke out your supply, use boxwood, cedar, Arbor vitae tips or evergreens from your foundation planting. Avoid hemlock, yew or spruce, greens that drop their needles. Using a good pruner, everything should be snipped into a pile of 6" pieces. Do this first.

Supplies are truly minimal. You will need a box-type four-ring wreath frame, 10" or 12" or larger if you prefer, and a spool of sturdy carpet thread in any neutral color. Wrap the wreath ring with left over scraps of ribbon you might have (big bows from gift boxes will do nicely) or strips of left-over materials cut on the bias with a pinking shears. Secure the beginning and ends of your wrappings with pins or staples.

Covering the wreaths frame first prevents light from passing through the completed dried wreath. Herbs are fleshy when fresh, thin leaved when dried, never heavy as pine cones or evergreens. As they dehydrate, dry and shrink, they lose their density. Wrapping the wire wreath ring is important but what you use to do so is immaterial since it doesn't show.

Start anywhere by knotting the thread securely. Lay a small handful of assorted herbs (6 or 10 stems) against the ring and tie them in place by wrapping the thread around the ring several times. Hold the spool firmly in your hand and bring it up through the center of the wreath form.

Place a similar bunch covering the stems of the preceeding bunch and wrap them in place by pulling the thread tightly as you work. Continue on around the ring in this manner until it is totally covered. Lay the bunches on quite thickly covering the base as much as possible. Where the first and last bunches of herbs join, you will place a bow so don't worry if it seems a little flat there.

The bunches can be as varied as you like using everything your garden yields. The loveliest wreath of all is entirely silver herbs if you have enough silver plants to do this. Ornamented with silvery lunaria, pearly everlasting, white feverfew flowers, baby's breath, and velvet bows in white, they are an elegant wedding decoration.

If all you have to work with is mint, an all mint wreath is certainly possible and this is usually the most fragrant of all. Enjoy sniffing your hands after making your wreath!

The next day, when your herbs begin to dry and shrivel, snip off drooping tips or any heavy steams that protude. Tuck in additional material if it seems necessary, it's easy to do.

Allow the wreath to dry several days in a warm dry place, preferably out of strong light and lying flat. The fragrance of the drying wreath is heavenly so place it where you can enjoy it during the process. Once it is dry, hang it on the kitchen wall to ornament it. And enjoy it.

Now your imagination can take over. If your herb garden has produced seed heads such as beebalm, hyssop, tansy buttons or golden yarrow, mint spikes, lavender flowers, the knotted marjorams, dill heads or any available dried flowers, gather all you can and poke them down into the wreath.

No need to wire the herbs on picks. They have sturdy stems which will be caught in the network of dried herbs and threads. You can't believe how easy this is to do until you have done it. If you want to include fragrant spices in your wreath, you will need to wire and tape these onto picks to insert them into the herbs and that is quite another matter. Sometimes they can be glued in place.

No herb garden? Herbs of the field and roadsides are free for the gathering. Golden rod, Joe-pye-weed, boneset, pearly everlasting, staghorn sumac, catnip, dock, Queen-Anne's-Lace, and many other wild herbs of the field are welcome additions. Tuck in strawflowers, "Fairy" roses if you have them available (use these fresh and let them dry on the wreath), eucalyptus and any other dried materials you might like to add to make your wreath as pretty and colorful as possible.

They can be all alike or each different, depending upon where you plan to use them and the materials you have available. It is best to group similar wreaths in the same general area. Harmonize them together with your "favorite things" theme, color scheme or identical bows.

A bow** will compliment and complete your herbal wreath. Make it full and perky, in white for the wedding then change it later to enhance a room or indicate a season. Your beautiful fragrant herb wreath decorations will be something you will enjoy for a long time after the wedding is over. It can be added to, refreshed and used for years.

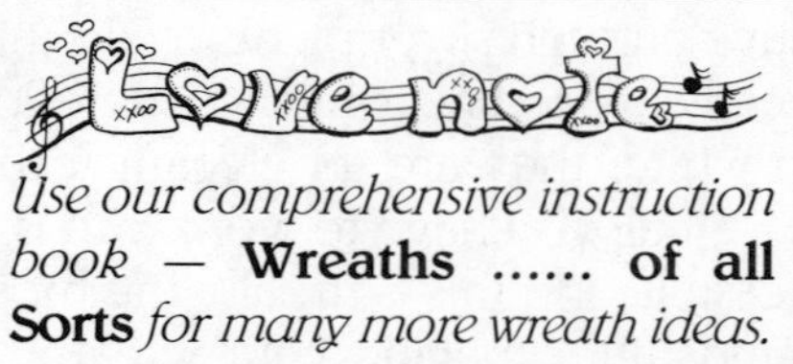

Use our comprehensive instruction book — **Wreaths ...... of all Sorts** *for many more wreath ideas.*

QUICKIE SPICE WREATHS

These adorable aromatic wreaths can be as small as favors or as large as decorations. Purchase styrofoam rings at any craft shop (or cut them out of cardboard) and wrap them with brown florist tape or textured fabric. Then devise and attach a small hanger.

Using tacky glue, cover your wreath generously with glue and then imbed bay leaves, small nuts, pinecones or acorns, bits of cinnamon bark, vanilla beans, whole aniseed, dill, cumin, caraway, poppyseeds

---

Madonna, wherefore hast thou sent to me
Sweet basil and mignonette?
Embleming love and health which never yet
In the same wreath might be.

— Percy Byshee Shelley

. . . anything dried from your herb garden or spice cupboard can be added. Whole cloves and star anise are both fragrant and attractive. For color, glue on cardamon, dried orange peel, petals, rosehips, candied ginger, pistachios, whatever is available. Look around you, especially at the spices in your favorite store, with an eye towards color, size, shape, and texture as well as fragrance.

A bow is your option. Allow your wreath to dry thoroughly before hanging. They are easy, charming and fragrant ornaments or favors. Styrofoam balls can be covered the same way then used as topiary decorations.

TRIM A WEDDING HAT

Straw hats trimmed with herbs and dried flowers are perfect accents for church or, especially, summer garden weddings. They are stunning yet easy to do.

For each hat you will need the following and about an hour of time.

Straw hat of your choice
1 yd. #9 satin ribbon
½ yd. #3 satin ribbon
small piece Spanish moss
colorful dried flowers and herbs, your choice
more ribbon for bow and streamer
about 3 yds. #9 satin ribbon
Tacky glue

Glue the yard of ribbon around the crown of the hat, allowing for long streamers in back. Tie the streamers using the narrow piece of ribbon. Because of the contour of the crown, the ribbon will not be smooth. No matter, it will be well covered. Dab glue on top of the hat band and pat moss in place. The moss gives you a textured bed in which to nestle your flower heads and herbs. Put glue in a small dish and one by one dab each piece in glue then into place around the crown. You can start with large flowers and feather it out on both sides towards the back or place small matching clusters in several equi-distant places or simply glue them hit-or-miss. Finally attach a pretty bow with more streamers in back.

SACHETS

When you use the French word SACHET you mean "in a little bag." The only difference between potpourri and sachet is just that. You have put some potpourri "in a little bag" or small sack.

FOR SACHET FAVORS, use a 6" square of organdy, satin, calico or tulle, in your choice of color. Pile potpourri in the center, draw up sides to surround a ball of potpourri and secure with a 12" piece of narrow ribbon. Tie a bow. Catch a little flower or sprig of rosemary in the bow. Arrange the corner points of the square into lively puffs. Made long in advance of the festivities, these can be stored in lidded boxes lined with tissue to preserve their fragrance until party time.

PAPER SACHETS are perfect for your paper anniversary. Fold colorful papers into packets holding strongly scented potpourri. Glue the sachets to paper lace doilies, round or square or both together, add tiny ribbons, floral seals and a dash of glitter. Reminiscent of old fashioned Valentines, these are fun to make and can be turned into invitations or favors.

KEEPSAKE SACHETS — Make them of lace, tulle, calico, or the fabric used to make the bridesmaids' dresses. Select herbs you plan to use in the wedding . . . roses, lavender, mint, sage, rosemary and so on. Combine the dried herbs together with oil and fixatives to make a fragrant potpourri** mixture to use in sachet favors at the rehearsal dinner for the close family and wedding party. Whether you stitch up little pillows or make your sachets out of 6" squares of material, tie them with a bow** and they will be adorable keepsakes.

Love note

"Lavender — 'to lay away the wedding gown.'" Store your treasured garment properly, for your children and your children's children. Professionals advise a dark, dry, cool or airy place. Have it cleaned so all dust is removed before it is laid away in acid proof blue tissue paper, lots and lots of it, then sealed in a lidded box. Before you seal it, however, flat sachet pillows filled with a pound of lavender blossoms (grown in your garden or purchased) will protect your cherished momento from moths, keeping it as fresh and fragrant as the day you said "I do."

SACHET CENTERPIECE — Select a graceful branch or branches and secure in a flower pot (or any container) with plaster of Paris. A few rocks in the bottom will stabilize your centerpiece by giving it weight. Stitch heart sachets of calico or lace, fill with fragrant potpourri and hang on the branches. They will grace your table and make delightful favors, too. Not good at stitchery? Buy metal tea balls, the kind you use to make a pot of tea, fill with potpourri and hang. Tie them on with little bows.

THE RING BEARER'S PILLOW, stuffed with fragrant potpourri, is a pretty sachet to use in the bride's linen closet. If a moth mixture is used, one including lots of lavender blossoms, it can be packed away with the wedding gown, a traditional protective sachet as well as an heirloom keepsake.

ICE CREAM CONE SACHETS. Buy real cones or devise a cornucopia from circular pieces of stiff papers. Make sachet balls by filling 6" squares of pastel fabric with 1/3 c. potpourri. Tie firmly into a plump rounded ball and insert it upsidedown into the cone, rounded side up. Fruit flavor oils are always a winner.

LOLLYPOP SACHETS — Small sachet balls can be bowed to lollypop sticks as novel favors. These are cute decorations tied to a Christmas tree.

SACHET NOSEGAYS — These sachets will require pipe cleaner stems to make fragrant giveaways. One large sachet ball centered in a round lacy paper doiley is a charming small souvenir. Or several smaller sachet balls, clustered together, is an attractive easy project. Complete the nosegays by adding bows with streamers.

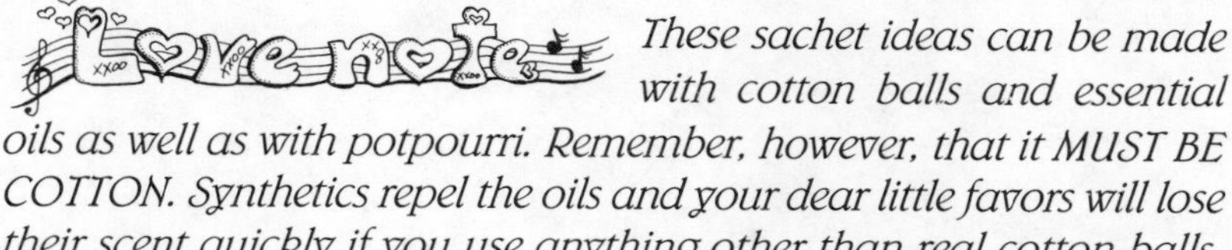

These sachet ideas can be made with cotton balls and essential oils as well as with potpourri. Remember, however, that it MUST BE COTTON. Synthetics repel the oils and your dear little favors will lose their scent quickly if you use anything other than real cotton balls.

VICKI'S HEART SACHETS

Love note

A dear clever friend has given us an original heart sachet, a simple little pattern that's worth its weight in gold. It is an easy to stitch heart sachet. Make these potpourri bags as gifts from the bride to her attendants. They can be filled with colors to match their dresses such as pink rosebuds, purple lavender, pale green lemon verbena, blue batchelor buttons, golden jasmine. Tie the bottoms with ribbon to match and — voila! — you have a pretty heart sachet, the most useful wedding party accessory you can make.

Vicki, a most talented seamstress, devised this easy-to-make heart which she has made by the hundreds of all kinds of materials.

MATERIALS FOR ONE HEART:
2 — 6 x 16" pieces of tulle, folded to 6" x 8"
18" of ½" lace
4" of ⅛" ribbon (loop)
12" of ⅛" ribbon (bow/tie)

1. Using a paper pattern, sew two folded tulle pieces together with a straight stitch: ½ inch seam, adding ribbon loop to center top. Start on the bottom folded edge and end at the opposite side, leaving the bottom open.
2. Sew lace on top of ½ inch seam with a slight zig zag stitch to within two inches of bottom edge. Miter lower edge of lace.
3. Stuff with potpourri.
4. Loosely baste bottom with six strand embroidery thread. Pull to gather and close. Conceal with a bow. Voila! A heart.

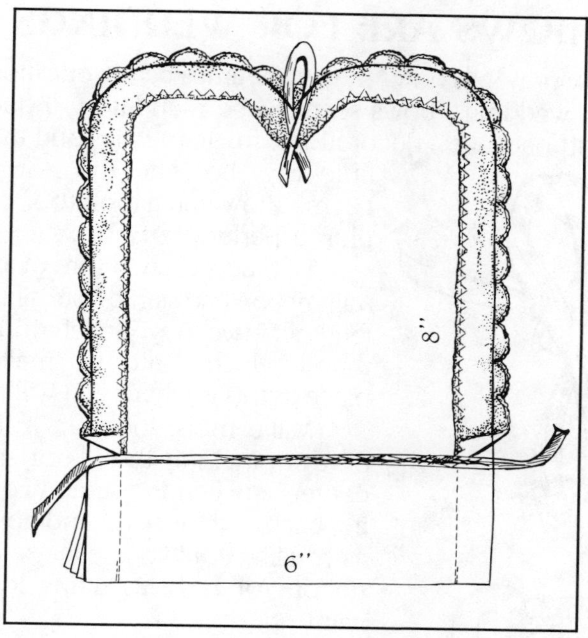

HELEN'S POP-UPS

This simple Pop-Up placecard can carry a name, a good luck wish, or an herb with its symbolism. Use pumpkins for fall, trees for Christmas, eggs for Easter or hearts any time. The card is best devised from sturdy white paper such as watercolor paper. The pop-up should be a contrasting color and is glued below the fold line on the bottom half. It can also be an invitation or clever thank you card. Once folded, it stands smartly at attention.

BOWS ARE FOR WEDDINGS

"To bow or not to bow" may sometimes be the question but when it comes to weddings, bows seem to be mandatory. Bouquets, centerpieces, gift packages, decorations, tussie-mussies and in a hundred little ways, bows are the crowning touch. Let me show you a foolproof way to make plump perky pretty bows.

To practice, cut a yard of any available satin ribbon and start by pressing a four inch length between your left forefinger and thumb. Pinch it into the smallest possible place as this is where you will tie the knot.

Make more loops in a figure eight, always pinching the "knot spot" in the center between the same two fingers, going back and forth, up and down, as often as you like until you have used up all your ribbons or have as many loops as you want.

Turn the ribbon as you work so the satin side (or velvet or calico) is always on the outside.

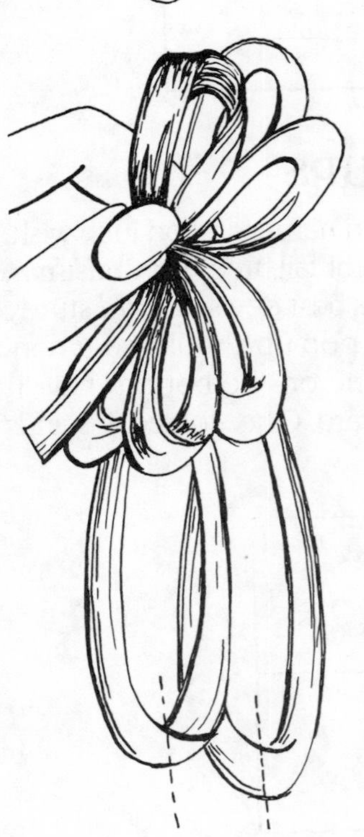

Using additional yards of ribbon, make a few extra long loops to tuck in as streamers, to dangle freely or these can also be cut.

Secure the pinched central "knot spot" with wire or pipecleaner or tie it in the center with another narrow piece of ribbon.

Bows can be made into full pompons by making eight or more loops on each side of the center pinched knot spot, all the same size.

You can, of course, graduate the bow loops from large to small in a formal effect; or they may be looped free form of any size into a more carefree bow.

Bows are fun to do. Practice over and over until you get the idea and see for yourself how easy it is to put a perky bow on everything. Finally trim the ends and streamers. Cut them straight across or in long elegant points or a birdtail "V." For the bride's bouquet, "tie the knot" in the streamer ends.

It's not finished until it has a BOW!

TRIM-A-HEART BASKET

To match the wedding hats (page 69), it's just as easy to ornament baskets for all attendants, flower girls or to hold rice or favors.

Dab glue along the top of your basket (white glue or use a glue gun) press Spanish moss in place, then imbed flowers, herbs and baby's breath in gay profusion. Adorn with a bow or two and you have completed more romantic wedding accessories.

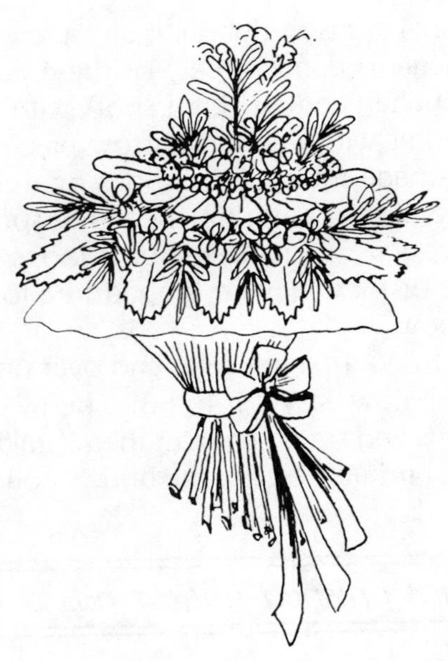

". . .A JOY FOREVER"

Or How to Preserve Your Wedding Bouquet

Beautiful flowers and a lovely bride are the combination that makes a wedding a thing of beauty. Photographs and gowns packed away in lavender are tangible momentos. But what of the perishable fragile wedding flowers? They are the stuff of which memories are made. Make them permanent keepsakes to treasure forever.

It's very satisfying to preserve the wedding flowers. Furthermore, you have a choice of ways to do it, none of them difficult. Use any or all of the methods suggested, depending upon the amount of flowers available.

Drying the wedding bouquet is the most popular. Arrange with your florist to have a small bouquet to toss so you can preserve your wedding herbs and flowers to decorate your first home.

If preserving the all-important wedding bouquet is your intention, then request flowers that are foolproof such as chrysanthemums, carnations, and roses. Gladiolus and orchids are extremely difficult to preserve but it can be done as long as you don't expect them to look as dewey-fresh as the original.

Since best results are achieved by working with the flowers and herbs as soon after the ceremony as possible, perhaps one of your attendants or a clever craft-minded relative will take care of this for you if the necessary equipment has been assembled before hand.

In drying flowers, there are several important things to remember. First, keep them dry; and second, get to the project as quickly as possible, before the flowers fade. If it cannot be done immediately, keep the flowers cool and dry, wrapped in plastic, in a refrigerator. With luck, they will keep well for up to a week.

To preserve them in third dimensional loveliness, you will need a box of silica gel — a commercial product with several trade names — and a tightly lidded can. Take apart the bride's bouquet reducing the stems to two inches. Boutonnieres, reception flowers, attendant's bouquets, church decorations and cake tops can be done the same way. Bury each flower in the silica gel, following instructions on the box. Seal the lid with masking tape and in less than a week your flowers will be dry and permanently preserved. Spray them with clear plastic or shellac to prevent shattering and the disastrous effects of humidity.

Another way to dry the flowers, use sterilized playbox sand available from hardware stores or building suppliers. Be sure it's playbox sand and not builder's sand which is too sharp and will cut the petals. Pour a layer of sand in a shoebox, carefully imbed the flower heads or herbs of your choice in the sand, and cover completely with another layer of sand. The flowers should not touch each other. After a week in a warm dry place, most flowers will be chip dry enough for fragile permanence behind glass.

They can then be re-assembled as they were or arranged in a container to ornament your new home or — my preference — placed in a frame under glass with the wedding announcement. No matter the degree of artistry, this thoughtful gift will be a favorite.

Preserve a treasured wedding announcement in a gold shadowbox frame, surround it with symbolic herbs and flowers and you've given the best of all possible gifts to a bride, new or old. Or to yourself.

On a pale background, perhaps a bit of the wedding dress if possible, the announcement and floral wreath are easily glued in place with any clear drying adhesive. Encircle the announcement with the dried flowers and herbs.

"HEARTS AND FLOWERS"

How to Press Herbs and Flowers

The secret to the successful pressing of flowers is an even distribution of weight on the books containing the flowers and — most important — frequently changing the absorbant papers between the flowers. I use white tissues or blotting paper which fill rapidly with moisture removed from the flowers. If the tissues are not changed, moisture will go back into the drying flowers, turning them very dark. As I said, for best color, change the absorbent papers every three days.

The nice part about pressed flowers is that if you forgot to do it in the summer, you can always buy a few flowers from the florist in winter and press them.

Some symbolic herbs to add are sage for domestic tranquility, lavender for luck, mint for joy, roses for love and rosemary for remembrance.

An interesting combination of five flowers selected from Selam, the *Oriental Language of Flowers*, would include the following: white lilacs to speak of the first dream of love; dogwood for faith and hope; the daisy which is a traditional good luck gift to a woman; pansies for a good luck gift to a man; clover blossoms to complete the circle of love and speak of fulfillment and fertility.

For the new bride, of course, you should use some of her very own wedding flowers along with the symbolic herbs. Most of them will dry quite readily using the above methods.

Certain "fat" flowers, such as roses, do not flatten very easily and for these you will have to remove outside petals to press separately. Daisies, bouvardia, stephanotis, violets and other thin petalled flowers are better subjects for pressing. Be sure to press some of the foliage, especially ferns. A flower press is nice but old telephone books are all you need, if they are well weighted.

How to "Petal Point" the Invitation

Any frame will work well with these, your wedding flowers, once pressed. Select a background, glue it into place with rubber cement and arrange the flowers in an attractive design. If the frame is large enough, you can include the wedding invitation, the bride's portrait, newspaper announcement of the engagement and such memorabilia, one or all, embroidered with the treasured flowers. After you have designed your composition to your satisfaction, use white glue to keep it in place, replace the glass and hang prominantly.

Every newly wedded household should have such a wall decoration, a gentle reminder for anniversaries to come. They make the most welcome of gifts, of course.

A BRIDAL POTPOURRI OF SCENT AND SENTIMENT

If you want to enjoy your flowers fresh and lovely for as long as possible (or if your wedding flowers are still in a box in the attic, a faded remnant of their once glorious role), you can always convert them into potpourri. In fact, any of the wedding flowers that aren't pressed or haven't dried successfully can be air dried and turned into the fragrant mixture called potpourri.

The ancient art of making potpourri lends itself to the preservation of traditional wedding flowers. It is a rich combination of scent and sentiment.

Starting with prom corsages if you wish, you can add other treasured flowers to your collection — engagement roses, shower centerpieces, Valentines. Later you can collect anniversary bouquets and, eventually, Mother's Day tributes. That's looking ahead!

Enjoy them first, then pull the faded flowers apart and don't overlook the foliage as you work. If they are not absolutely dry, spread them out on a clean sheet of paper and let the air complete the work for you. They MUST be completely dry.

When the petals feel crunchy to the touch ("chip-dry" we call it) go to your nearest herb shop to obtain a little bottle of essential oil and some orris root, a modest investment.

The orris root will act as a fixative for the fragrances and the oil of your choice will make your wedding flowers smell heavenly. Add approximately ¼ cup orris root to a quart of petals and six to 12 drops (or more) of oil, combine and stir; place in a covered container to blend and mellow; stir occasionally over a period of a month or so, adding dried orange peel, spices, your wedding herbs, or more oil if you want to increase the fragrance. Placed in an attractive covered jar, your wedding flowers will perfume your room and your life whenever you wish.

Open your fragrant jar of wedding flowers to release its perfume; close it when not in use so it will be preserved and the fragrance renewed for all the years of your marriage.

Wedding flowers, as all living things, are, alas, perishable. But don't let that deter you. Keep your beautiful flowers for as long as you like — dried, pressed or in fragrant potpourri — a timeless keepsake to cherish and an heirloom for the future.

A Bride's Basic Potpourri

1 quart rose petals or scented herbs, dried
3 tablespoons orris root powder
8 drops rose oil

Combine all the above; place in a tightly covered plastic container for several weeks; stir occasionally; add more oil if you wish it to be stronger. Put the finished product in a pretty jar to enjoy for many years.

A Forty Year Old Rose Jar Recipe

Rose petals (or wedding flowers)
¼ ounce cloves, mace, and allspice
½ ounce cinnamon
2 ounces powdered orris root
¼ pound lavender flowers
¼ ounce toilet water or cologne (perferably lavender)
a few drops of rose oil

Dry rose petals and mix with ¼ cup of salt. Stir the above spices, lavender flowers, toilet water, oil and orris root into the dried rose petals. Age in a tight tin for several weeks before putting it in a decorative container to perfume the new home.

Grow old along with me!
The best is yet to be,
The last of life, for which the first was made....

— Robert Browning

"From this day forward" Wedding Potpourri

"Gather some of the flowers from the wedding party, the reception, the church flowers, her own bouquet if possible, the boutonnaires, corsages worn by the mothers — every flower that is incorporated in the wedding itself is to be dried, saved and treasured. Even if the flowers are given no special attention but left in the original bouquets they will air dry satisfactorily. And who will deny that in 25 years they will be the jewels of her memories."

from *POTPOURRI: RECIPES AND CRAFTS*
by Pat Humphries and Bertha Reppert
Another Remembrance Press Publication

My Favorite Potpourri

1 quart dried wedding herbs and flowers
½ cup patchouli
¼ cup sandlewood chips
¼ cup vetiver roots
1 teaspoon frankincense and myrrh
1 teaspoon powdered cloves
1 teaspoon powdered cinnamon
1 tonka bean, chopped fine
¼ cup allspice
10 drops rose oil
1 cup orris root

Mix everything together. The oil and orris can be mixed together and added last. Stir. Store in a closed jar for 2-4 weeks until well blended. Put in a pretty jar for your living room. Open and stir to enjoy the fragrance of your wedding herbs and flowers.

Dear, dear doctor,
What will cure love?
Nothing but the clergy,
And white kid glove.

BRIDE'S HEELS

Here's a vintage touch for a wedding, pure Victoriana. Make a pair of white satin, cotton padded, heel pads for the bride's slippers, to be worn on her wedding day. (See pattern.) Embroider or paint lily-of-the-valley around the edge. Put the bride's initials, month and day of the wedding on the left heel; groom's initial, and year, on the right heel. On each heel put a four leaf clover. Be sure to put sachet in each heel then blanket stitch around the edge (moss green is a pretty color). Making bride's heels may take all day but they are a highly personal gift or keepsake. "Here comes the bride . . ." tum tum ta tum . . . .

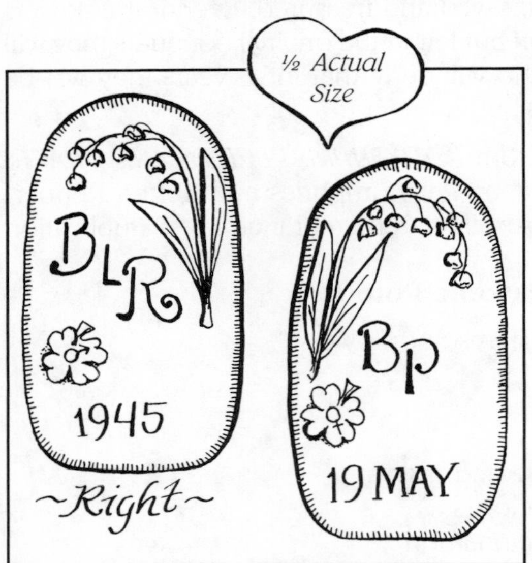

LAWN HERBS FOR LUCK. Three leafed clovers are so important to weddings and matters of the heart that St. Valentine could be jealous. Symbolizing a prosperous joyous long marriage with great happiness and good fortune, clovers also offer substantial protection to the household. No bride should go down the aisle without clovers of love in both shoes!

POTPOURRI PARASOLS

For each parasol or shower favor, you will need:

2 calico material squares, cut to pattern
1-4" length and 1-11" length of ½" lace and coordinating thread
1 pipecleaner (12")
¼ cup fragrant potpourri

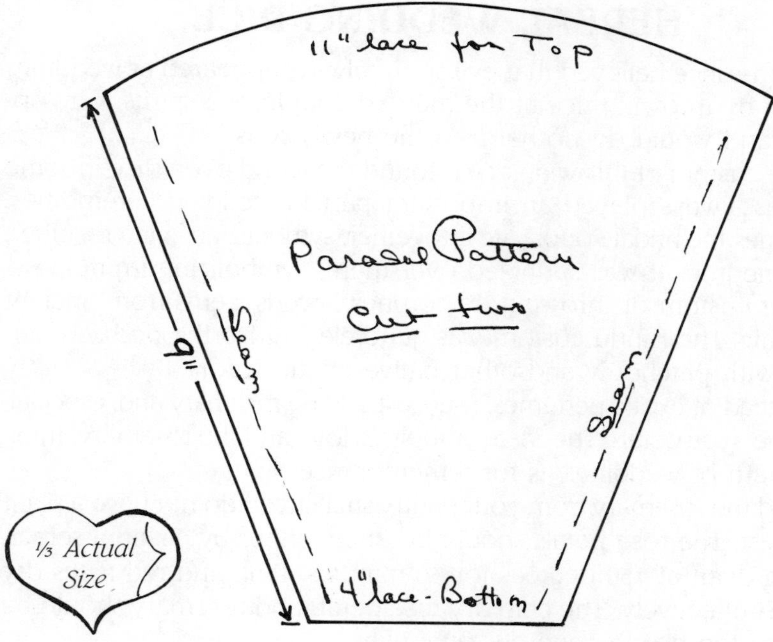

To prepare the parasol shower favor:

1. With wrong sides together, stitch ¼" side seams. Turn right side out and press.
2. Hand or machine stitch 11" length of lace around the top edge (lace ruffles upward). Hand stitch the 4" length of lace around the bottom edge (lace ruffles downward). Be careful not to stitch the parasol closed!
3. Insert pipe cleaner down the middle of the parasol with approx. 2-3" showing out the bottom. Stitch in place, across the bottom.

4. Gather the bottom with basting stitches and pull closed. Secure with tiny stitches.
5. Stuff the parasol with your favorite potpourri.
6. Baste the top closed, gather and hand stitch, secure with tiny stitches. Tie the narrow satin bow in place, just below the lace edge.
7. Bend the upper portion of the pipecleaner to form handle.

HERBAL WEDDING RICE

It was once believed that evil spirits always appeared at weddings and that by throwing rice at the married couple, the spirits were appeased and would do no harm to the newlyweds.

The custom of throwing rice is found the world over. Rice in some form has always played an important part in wedding ceremonies. Sometimes the bridal couple ate it together, symbolizing living together; and sometimes it was sprinkled over them, symbolizing fruitfulness.

Our custom of throwing rice on newlyweds stems from ancient Hindu law. The Hindu custom was quite elegant for the rice was perfumed with patchouly and other native exotic scents.

Instead of exotic perfumes, I suggest adding rosemary and, especially in June, rose petals. The rose symbolizes love and the rosemary, traditional herb of weddings, is for remembrance.

Add the rosemary from your pantry shelf if you do not have a plant to harvest. The rose petals should be dried, either by air on a screen or in an oven at 150 degrees for 30 minutes. Pink and red roses dry the most effectively. The chip dry rose petals and rosemary should be added to the rice in generous quantities.

A large bowl of the wedding rice mixture can be placed where the guests can help themselves to a handful. It is also prettily presented in individual packets of net or organdy tied with ribbons that harmonize with the wedding colors. A young sister or two would be happy to hold a basket of the rice packages at the church. Tie a bunch of herbs on the handle of the basket.

Your guests will be enchanted by the colorful and fragrant addition of rosemary and rose petals. The ancient symbolism will annoint the newly-weds with all kinds of beautiful good wishes. We like to attach little cards to the individual rice packets.

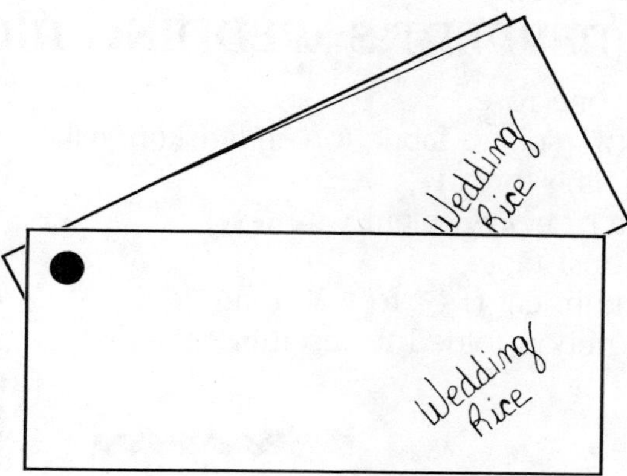

You could cook and serve this wedding rice, you know, since both roses and rosemary are edible.

If there are objections to throwing rice for one reason or another, simply substitute bird seed and our feathered friends will clean it up while they feast.

To color wedding rice, use vegetable dye food coloring of your choice. Make a glass full of a deep colored solution and pour it over the white rice. Strain and reuse the dye bath until you have done as much colored rice as desired. It's amazing how quickly the dry rice absorbs color. Dry the rice thoroughly on thick newspapers before adding herbs or packaging.

NANCY REPPERT'S WEDDING RICE ROSES

Materials for one rose:

- 4½" x 4½" square fabric (organdy, satin, calico, etc.)
- coordinating thread
- 8" piece of heavyweight wire (#26)
- green florist tape
- green cloth leaf (1½" to 2½" long) (or ribbon folded to resemble a leaf)

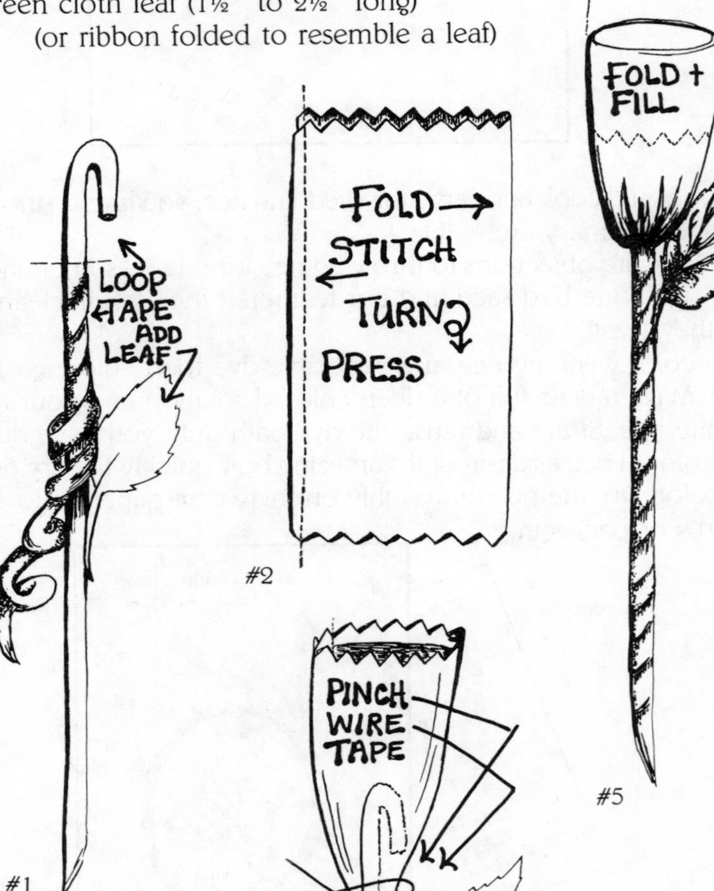

1. Prepare the wire stem for each rose by forming a ¼" loop at the top of the wire. Beginning just below the loop, completely cover the stem with florist tape, pulling and stretching the tape as you go, releasing the adhesive from the tape. Halfway down the stem, begin to attach the leaf to the stem, taping both together. For variety, attach the leaves at various locations on the wire stem.
2. To prepare the body of the rose, fold the 4½" x 4½" piece of fabric in half, right sides together. Stitch the length of the 4½" side, forming a tube. Turn the material right side out. Press. Factory: Sew'm all in one row — back stitch then snip apart!
3. To attach the tube to the prepared stem, insert the looped end of the wire into the base of the tube. Not too far! Pinch the base tightly and using very short stitches, secure the material to the wire.
4. With the florist tape, cover the gathered material and stitches securing them to the stem.
5. On the top of the rose, fold a ¼" hem inward; forming a pocket. Fill the pocket with WEDDING RICE WITH ROSEBUDS AND ROSEMARY (page 84) — or Bird Seed.
6. For presentation, poke the roses into a basket with styrofoam on the bottom to help stabilize the roses and prevent the contents from spilling. If you are making these well in advance of the wedding, after filling the roses tuck a small piece of paper towel in the top to prevent spilling. Remember to remove the papers prior to presenting the roses to the wedding guests.

Love note

Nancy suggests:

A. A basket of these roses makes an easy dual purpose centerpiece for any bridal party including the reception.

B. Make half "his" color and half "her" color and pass them out to "his" and "her" family and friends at the church.

C. An informal committee can make dozens of wedding rice roses well in advance, another "fun" party.

BRIDE'S FAN SHAPED RING PILLOW

This different little ring pillow is simple to make and could be made in material that matches the bride's gown. It is a lovely handmade keepsake.

Materials:

satin or moire fabric (2 pieces, 8½" x 8")
2 yards white ribbon
18" ruffled white lace
7 white flowers (or ribbon roses)
cotton stuffing (or potpourri)

Cut two pieces of fabric following the pattern. Sew two straight sides together with right sides facing. Turn to right side and sew on stitching lines to create the divisions of the "fan." Stuff each section, then turn in curved edge and hand sew with tiny stitches. Stitch ruffled lace along curved edge. Tack on white flowers. Tack a small piece of ribbon to center of pillow so that ring may be loosely attached. Attach ribbon carefully to bottom of fan with hanging streamers. Dab a bit of perfume oil on the back of the padded "fan."

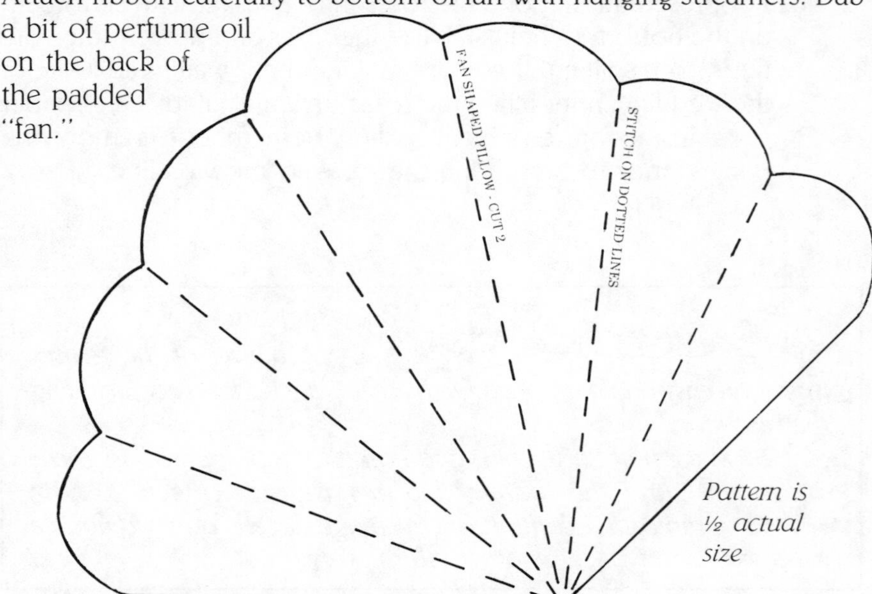

RIBBON ROSES

Make a right angle fold in the center of a 30" piece of ribbon. Fold ends back and forth, as shown, to the ends of the ribbon.

Hold ends and release folds. Now grasp just one end (A) and release the other. Pull slowly on free end until first or beginning fold almost disappears into center of flower. Tie ends together with thread or fine wire, which becomes your stem. Add a velvet rose leaf, if available, and tape the stem with florists' tape.

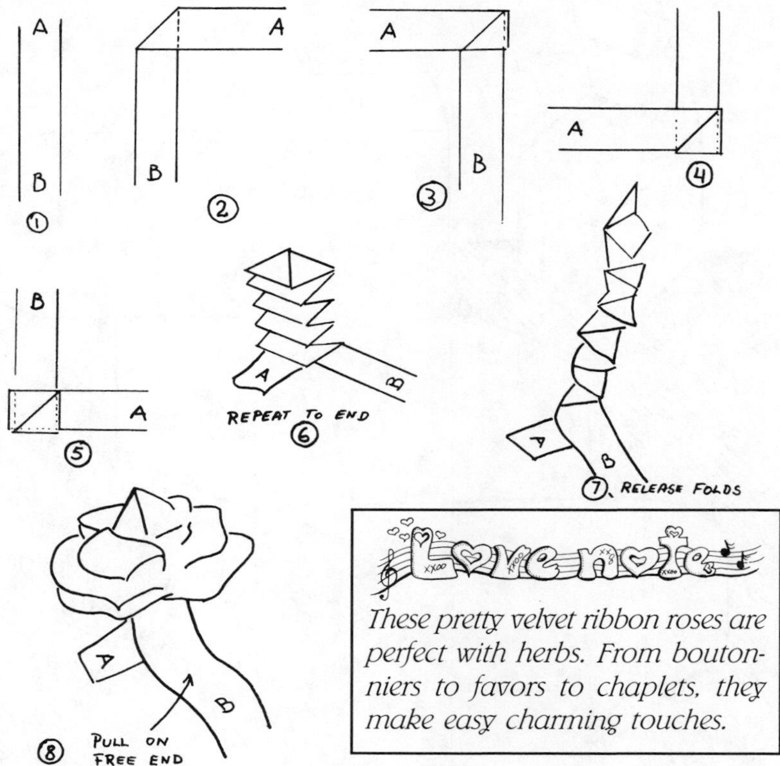

These pretty velvet ribbon roses are perfect with herbs. From boutonniers to favors to chaplets, they make easy charming touches.

Combine ribbon roses, laces, ribbons, dried flowers and herbs into a VICTORIAN FANTASY. Add anything — birds and butterflies, buttons and bows. Wrap the cluster in vintage crocheted doilies or velvet. Pin this romantic bouquet on broad brimmed hats, fans, muffs, baskets or vine wreaths. These irresistible wedding accessories are endlessly useful. A drop of essential oil here and there brings the cluster to life.

LITTLE BOXES

Little boxes can be useful for cake, rice, potpourri, birdseed, favors of many sorts. Easy to make, here's an old grade school pattern to guide you. Use plain white sturdy paper that can be decorated or not, as you wish. Or turn the project over to children who would like to participate in the wedding preparations.

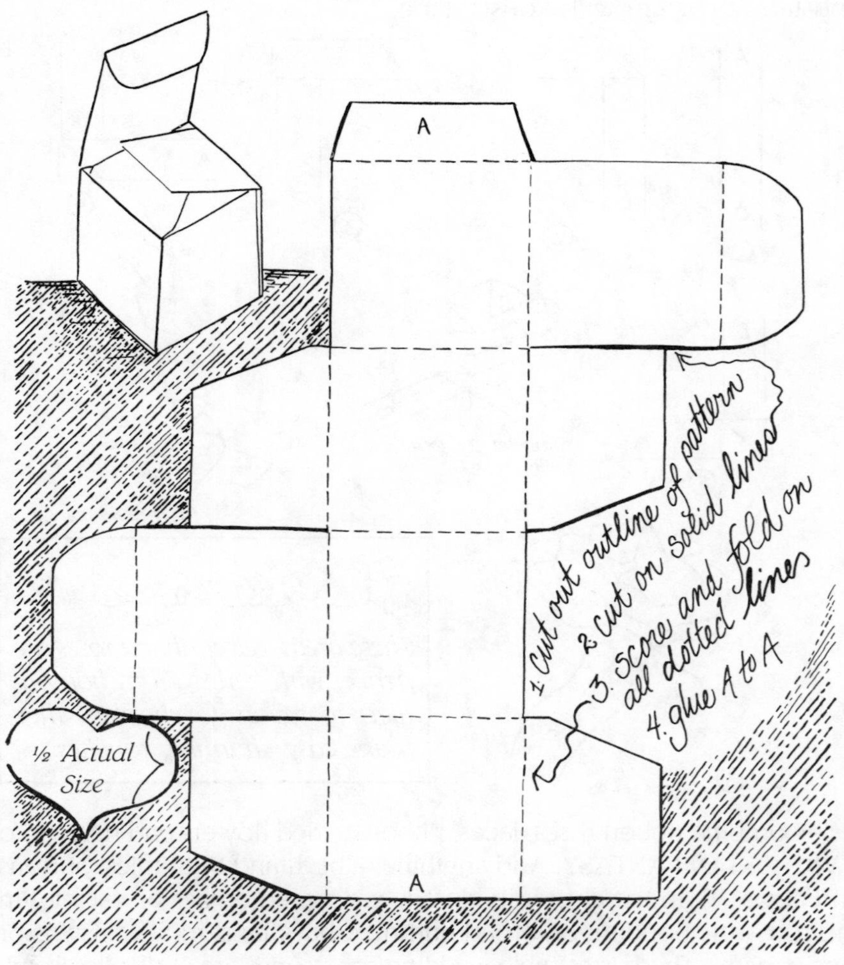

SHOWER INVITATION

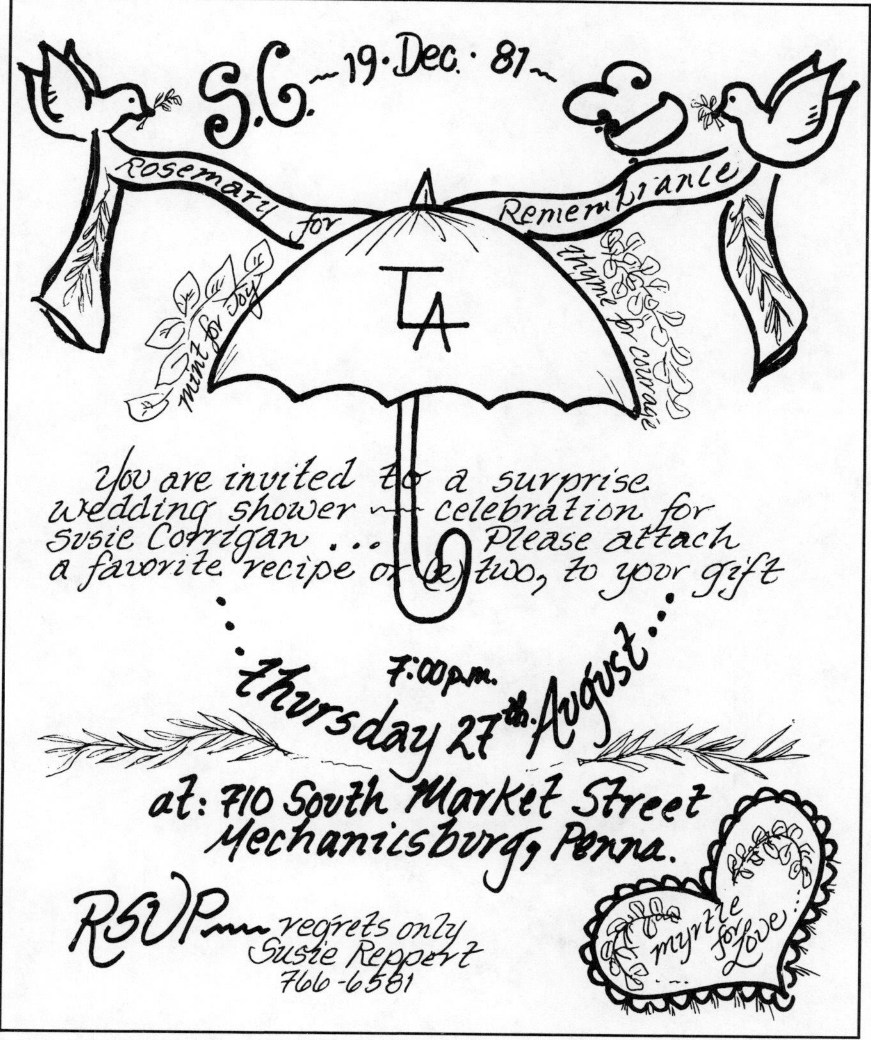

No herbal invitations available at your stationery store? No pressed herbs to create your own? No time for such handwork? Photocopy and use this handmade invitation. Use a piece of tracing paper to draw your own version, filling in appropriate names, date and place. It can be enlarged to 8½ x 11, folded and mailed without an additional envelope.

SYMBOLISM Sundry Herbs and Lovesome Flowers

A Bride's Bouquet

Here's Thyme to give you courage
Rosemary for the past
Sweet Lavender, a loyal heart
Yarrow, a love to last ~
Sage for a life that is long and
brave
Mint to quicken the brain
Violets to ward off evil ones
Basil to cure the pain and then for
fun and fragrance,
Southernwood will do.
Rose and Lemon and Ginger
mean a Sixpence in your shoe.

WEDDING CHARMS

"Something old,
Something new;
Something borrowed,
Something blue."

In English they add — "And a sixpence in her shoe." Wearing some piece of clothing from an older woman who is happily married is meant to transfer that good fortune to the new bride. It is a form of "sympathetic magic." Traditionally, the something borrowed should be golden because gold indicated the sun, the source of life.

Orange blossoms are used traditionally by brides because they come from an evergreen tree and therefore are believed to stand for everlasting love. Because the tree has the ability to blossom and fruit at the same time, it is considered particularly lucky. In Europe, brides once wore wreaths of grains or wheat, both emblems of fertility, to insure large families.

Wedding veils are a custom taken from the Far East, where because of the custom of Purdah, women wear covering to conceal all but their eyes until marriage. It is also supposed to be symbolic of the canopy once held over the bridal couple to protect them from the "evil eye."

Love note *As with other bridal fashions, there have always been cycles of favor for various bridal flowers. But since the orange blossom has enjoyed a full century of popularity, it may be interesting to know something about this delicate beautiful flower.*

Carried from Spain to America by Columbus' second voyage, the orange tree is one of the wonders of nature, bearing fruits and flowers all year long and at the same time. Because of this, the orange blossom has come to symbolize the young and fruitful bride.

Incredibly sweet, the fragrance of orange blossoms can be overpowering. The essential oil (called Neroli) is perfect for bridal potpourri. Orange blossom traditions became so strong the flowerlets were molded in wax when fresh blossoms were unobtainable.

Let this Rosmarinus, the flower of men, the ensigne of your wisdom love and loyaltie be carried not only in your hands, but in your heads and harts

Robert Hackett 1607

The bride's bouquet is usually decorated with ribbons in which the knots are tied. Because wishes were supposed to be held by a knot, many knots were needed to hold all the good wishes from the bride's friends. The lover's knot has been a marriage emblem from remotest times. It stood for love and duty. The actual tying together of two pieces of cord or ribbon at the marriage ceremony is an old Danish custom which spread to Holland and England. The knot was symbolic of oneness or unity. Today's expression "the knot was tied" means a marriage has taken place.

When the bride tosses her bouquet, the girl catching it will be the next one married according to another old tradition. She must make a wish for the bride's good fortune which will come true only if she unties one of the knots in the bouquet ribbons. In France, instead of her bouquet, the bride throws out a fancy garter. Whoever catches it will be married within a year.

Combine with herbs as many of these ancient lucky charms, amulets and symbolic customs as appeal to you to make your wedding that much more memorable.

A love potion made of a certain number of red and white rose petals and forget-me-nots, boiled in 385 drops of water for the sixteenth part of an hour, will, if properly made, insure the love of the opposite sex, if three drops of the mixture are put into something the person is to drink.

Old Charm

BLESS THE BRIDE

In England, Culpeper House sells a mixture of dried herbs and spices called "Bless the Bride with natural confetti." Associated with love and happiness, it contains rose buds 'pure and lovely,' orange blossoms 'bridal festivities,' peppermint 'warmth of feeling,' marjoram 'blushes,' parsley 'festivity,' fennel 'worthy of all praise,' sweet basil 'good wishes,' mugwort 'happiness,' rosemary 'remembrance,' sage 'domestic virtue,' "with a touch of cornflower (bachelors' button') to remind the groom it's all over now!" The colorful throwing mixture is also fragrant.

ANGELICA

The "herb of the angels" — John Parkinson wrote in the 17th century "The whole plant, both leafe, roote and seede, is of an excellent comfortable sent, savour and taste."

SEVEN BLESSING HERBS

1. ROSEMARY — Bless this wedding!
2. BAY — Bless the groom!
3. MYRTLE — Bless the bride!
4. FENNEL — Bless the baby!
5. CATNIP — Bless the kitty!
6. BASIL — Bless this home!
7. ANGELICA — Bless us all!

All dear Nature's children sweet
Lie 'fore bride and bridegroom's feet,
Blessing their sense!. . .

— John Fletcher's "Bridal Song"

THE WEDDING POUCH

Here's an oldie but goodie . . . Stitch up a small drawstring pouch to pin to the hem of the bridal gown.

It contains her insurance policy!

a piece of bread (food)
a scrap of cloth (clothes)
a sliver of wood (shelter)
a dollar bill (money)

I would also add a sprig of rosemary — "brings luck to marriage."

HERBS OF HAPPINESS (taken from an Avon tile created in England). "Every flower has its special meaning. Coreopsis is Ever Cheerful. Larkspur and Yellow Lily are Lighthearted. Chinese Chrysanthemum brings Merriment. Butterfly Orchids express Joy and Lily of the Valley celebrates the Return of Happiness.

A WREATH OF IVY encircles the bride's and groom's dinner plate at the reception to set them apart as guests of great honor and to symbolize "fidelity." Tuck in a few sprigs of sage as well "to insure domestic tranquility."

PIKAKE (Arabian jasmine) or (Jasminum sabue): In Hawaii, a little white, very sweet smelling flowers, with nine or ten petals, are used to make lovely Pikake leis. Pikake means "Peacock." If you have heavenly perfumed Pikake or jasmine flowers, use them in wedding work. If you have enough available, string the bride a fragrant lei for "love and luck."

THE ROYAL WEDDING PLATE created by Mary Grierson for the Franklin Mint of London to commemorate the marriage of Prince Charles and Lady Diana Spencer includes the following flowers, permanently captured on bone china by Royal Doulton, now a collector's item.

Pink roses to represent purity and loveliness
Pinks to speak of pure and ardent love
Violets as a promise of faithfulness
Forget-me-nots to tell of a love that is true
Primroses to express elegance and grace
Heartsease, the wild pansy that proclaims "My thoughts are always with you."

Brides, says the Society of American Florists, carry lilies-of-the-valley to illustrate the return of happiness; ivy to signify wedded bliss, and orchids to express beauty and refinement. A bit of heather may be added for luck, or asters as the talisman of love, is their advice to florists.

WEDDING HERBS GLOSSARY

(Includes herbs mentioned in the text.)

Alyssum, Sweet .... Worth beyond beauty
Amaranth .... Immortality
Ambrosia .... Love returned
Angelica .... Herb of the Angels
Inspiration, Protection
Apple Blossom .... Preference
Arbor vitae .... Unchanging friendship; the Tree of Life
Artemisias (all varieties) .... Everlasting; silvery grays for wreaths
Balm, Lemon .... Comfort
Basil, Sweet .... Good wishes
Bay Laurel .... Victory
Bay Wreath .... Reward of Merit, triumph, victory
Borage .... Courage
Boxwood .... Endurance
Broom .... Neatness
Burnet .... For a merry heart
Caraway .... Retention
Cedar .... Strength
Celandine .... Joys to come
Chamomile .... Energy in adversity
Chrysanthemum .... Cheerfulness
Cloves .... Dignity
Clover, Four-leaf .... Good Luck!
Clover, Red .... Industry
Clover, White .... Promise
Coriander .... Hidden worth
Corn .... Riches
Crocus, Spring .... Youthful gladness
Cumin .... Engagement
Daffodil .... Regard
Daisy .... Innocence; Hope
Dill .... Powerful against witchcraft
Dock .... Patience
Edelweis .... Devotion; Courage
Fennel .... Strength
Fern .... Fascination
Flax .... Domestic industry

Forget-me-not .... Forget-me-not
Geranium, Rose scented .... Preference
Gillyflower .... Bonds of affection
Hawthorne .... Hope; Charm against witchcraft
Heliotrope .... Devotion; Eternal love
Holly .... Foresight
Honestry (Lunaria) .... Money in your pocket
Honeysuckle .... Generous and devoted affection
Hyacinth, white .... Fertility
Hyssop .... Cleanliness
Iris .... A Message
Ivy .... Fidelity
Jasmine, white .... Sweet love
Jasmine, yellow .... Passionate love
Johnny-Jump-Ups .... "Heartsease"
Juniper .... Protection
Lavender .... Luck
Lemon .... Zest
Lilac .... Joy of youth
Lily-of-the-Valley .... Sweetness
Linden blossoms .... Conjugal love
Marjoram .... Joy
Meadowsweet .... Once considered the true wedding herb; for strewing
Mignonette .... Quiet sweetness
Mint .... Virtue
Mugwort .... Traveller's joy
Mustard Seed .... Faith
Myrtle .... True love
Nasturtium .... Patriotism
Olive .... Peace
Orange Blossoms .... Young purity
Oregano .... Joy of the mountain
Pansy .... Thoughts
Parsley .... Festivity
Peppermint .... Warm feelings
Pinks .... Always lovely
Queen Ann's Lace .... Queen of the meadow
Rose, Bridal .... Happy Love
Rose, White .... Youth and Beauty; Charm; Innocence
Rose, Red .... Desire; Love

Rosemary .... Remembrance
Rue .... Protection from evil
Sage .... Domestic virtue, health
Strawflowers Statice, etc. .... Forever yours
Southernwood (Lad's love) ..... Jest, Fun
Thyme .... Emblem of courage
Tulip, red .... Declaration of love
Valerian .... Accommodation
Verbena, lemon .... The herb of Venus, Unity
Vervain .... Enchantment
Violet .... Faithfulness
Wheat .... Modesty, Prosperity
Willow .... Freedom
Woodruff, Sweet .... For garlands
Wormwood .... Absence
Yarrow .... Everlasting love
Zinnia .... Missed in absence

THE SENTIMENTAL GARDEN

"There is a language, little known,
Lovers claim it as their own.
Its symbols smile upon the land,
Wrought by Nature's wonderous hand;
And in their silent beauty speak,
Of life and joy, to those who seek
For Love Divine and sunny hours
In the language of the flowers."

— J.S.H., from *The Language of Flowers*, London, 1875.

Herbs were used in so many ways down through the centuries that people began to endow them with even greater attributes. Because of their versatility of uses and effect upon people, the mysterious ways in which they could heal, their magical properties, real or imagined, herbs became a form of communication, an expression of love, victory, or sentiment suitable to all occasions, proper to religious ceremonies and affairs of state. Herbs became symbolic . . . (and) nosegays became the love letters of the day.

taken from *A Heritage of Herbs*
by Bertha Reppert (1976)

WEDDING HERBS

G. Milek ©1987

Globe Amaranth
everlasting love
Sage
domestic virtue
Thyme
courage-strength
Nigella
love-in-the-mist

Lavender
love — devotion
Rosemary
remembrance
Majoram
joy — happiness
Rose
love — desire

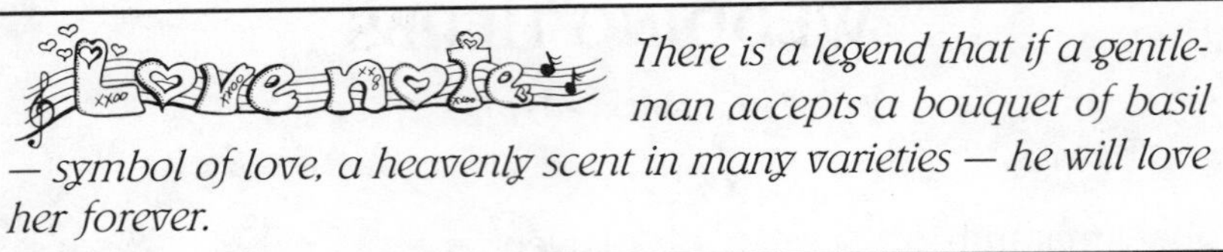

There is a legend that if a gentleman accepts a bouquet of basil — symbol of love, a heavenly scent in many varieties — he will love her forever.

SYMBOLISM BIBLIOGRAPHY

Flowers and Herbs of Love by Roy Genders (1978); Darton, Longman and Todd (England)

The Ladies' Flora by John G. Newman (1854); L.L. Boardman & Co. (London)

Language of Flowers illustrated by Kate Greenaway; Merrimack Publishing Corp. (N.Y.C.)

"Amur omnia vincit"

WONDERFUL RECIPES and SERVING TIPS

"WHAT SHALL I SERVE AT THE PARTY?"

Down the primrose path of four decades of matrimony and cooking, while raising a hungry brood and entertaining in our various homes, I have collected a certain number of tried and found to be true recipes. You may well have your own family favorites but let me share some of mine with you. The emphasis in all these Reppert recipes is on herbs.

Please adjust amounts any way you like, adopt them as your own. This collection is the backbone of a good party file. Many of these old favorites are easily made in advance for gracious carefree entertaining.

While planning your showers, luncheons, the reception, or a simple afternoon tea and open house to meet the engaged couple, create a real party atmosphere. Set your stage by developing an ambiance. Use a theme, a color scheme, lighting, music and a bower of herbs with flowers. Your party, well herbed, will be the talk of the town.

ENTERTAIN WITH MIRRORS! For a stunning effect, place food, candles, centerpieces and pots of herbs on mirrors of assorted sizes and shapes or the 12" decorator squares available for walls and ceilings. It will mirror everything dramatically, making your party look twice as good with half the effort.

CANDLES add their own charm. An inexpensive centerpiece is four vigil light candles on a mirror, with or without flowers. Colored glass containers of any kind sparkle like stained glass when the candles are lighted. A drop of essential oil in each will perfume the air.

Love note

SCENTED WASH UPS: Borrow an idea from any good Japanese restaurant . . . serve heated wet handcloths as a wash-up for "finger lickin' good" foods. Easy enough to do, wet and roll up inexpensive washrags or terry cloth squares hours in advance of your party. Refrigerate until needed.

After the ribs, chicken or corn-on-the-cob has been served and eaten, pop the attractively arranged basket of wet cloths into your microwave for two mintues. Presto! You are passing around toasty warm wipe-ups grateful guests will appreciate.

Not herbal? Oh, yes. That's your touch. Soak the cloths in water to which a drop of lemon oil has been added. Or roll the wet napkins around a sprig of fresh lemon balm from your herb garden.

WHEN IT'S YOUR TURN TO ENTERTAIN

After the honeymoon and settling in is over, plan an "AT HOME" party. An "Open House" especially over a holiday is an easy way to return many social obligations. Pick a day (Sunday) then limit the time (4 p.m. to 7 p.m.), send out herbal invitations and use this book to plan your first party.

Now it's your turn to create a party! Menus and decorations are fun to organize on paper. Put down all your favorite ideas then look it over carefully, decide what's realistic, cross off the impossible and proceed with your plans. Soft lighting, candles, bowls of potpourri everywhere, background music, flowers, herbs, wedding gifts and a theme will provide a pleasant environment for your party and ensure success.

Having someplace to go is home.
Having someone to Love is family.
Having both is a blessing.

This is the perfect opportunity to show the videotape of the wedding and reception. Did you tell the photographer, in advance, to zoom in on your special herbal touches?

A BOUNTIFUL BUFFET

To have an absolutely smashing party, concentrate your efforts on the presentation of the food you are serving. The eye feasts first. Lay down your tablecloth then elevate areas of your table or server with sturdy cartons. Now layer small cloths, snowy white, or matching napkins, or pieces of colorful materials over the cartons.

Serve your foods at various levels, reachable of course. Tuck fruit, vegetables, flowers in water picks and, naturally, bunches of herbs here and there.

If it's winter, pots of herbs or bunches of supermarket parsley and cress will work. Flowering kale is spectacular.

Gather apothecary jars of spices, long cinnamon sticks, colorful dried flowers and add them too. Tuck in country look animals, Grandmother's antiques, or your favorite small dolls. This can go on and on and on but I'm sure you get the idea. Crowded clutter decoratively arranged is the look you want to achieve. The motto is "and just one more!"

Little twinkly lights from Christmas are a striking addition. Add small vigil lights (even if it's a breakfast party, no matter). Now light your candles, mist the flowers and herbs gently, and call in your guests.

The superabundance of your presentation of tasteful things will overwhelm your party guests who will remember it forever. Don't be timid, trust me.

Love note *Such a bountiful buffet can be made seasonal by adding a collection of Valentine hearts, Easter rabbits, or the family Clauses. Use mirrors, too, to double the effect, an even more wonderful picture.*

THE BRIDE'S TABLE NAPKINS

Elegantly flaring linen napkins are the hallmark of the world's most exclusive dining rooms. A well folded napkin can set the scene for all your bridal parties, a conversation piece as well as another way to enjoy the presence of herbs.

Choose one of the ways shown here to fold your crisp linens, impeccable white or colored, place it in a tall wine or water goblet (to be filled after seating). Making it yet more impressive, top it off with a sprig or two of herbs.

Napkins also may be rolled singly as a scroll then tied with ribbons in the colors of the wedding party. Catch a perky sprig of rosemary in the bow.

Thus presented, parsley, sage, rosemary, or thyme will embellish your luncheon or the head table at the wedding. Use water picks (florists use these to give an individual flower its own supply of water) and well conditioned herbs of your choice. Your guests can take them along home.

It might be fun to consider "the guardian herbs," each labeled, of course.

Rose ....Guardian of True Love
Tansy ....Guardian of the Garden
Basil ....Guardian of the Loving Heart
Southernwood ......Guardian of the Closet
Rosemary ....Guardian of Friendship
Sage ....Guardian of Health
Bay ....Guardian of the House
Parsley ....Guardian of the Table
Daisy ....Guardian of Innocence and Secrets

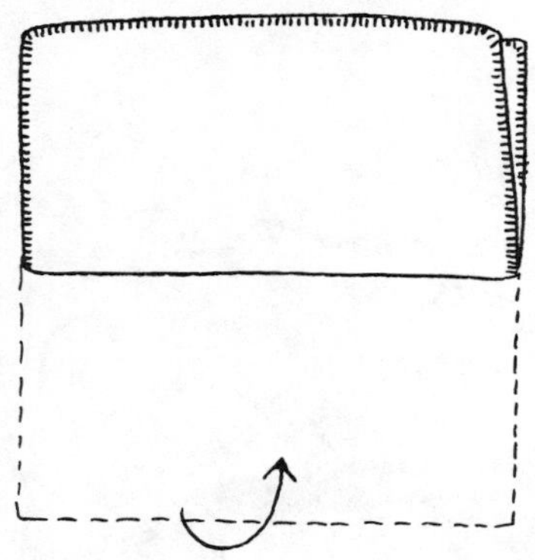

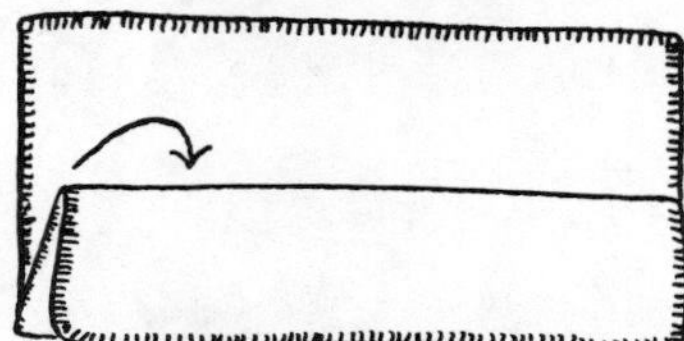

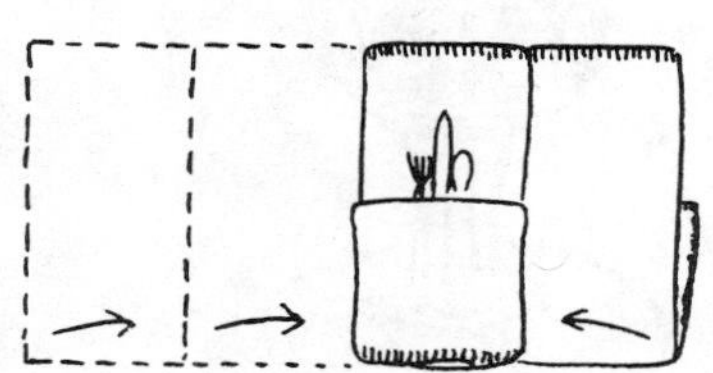

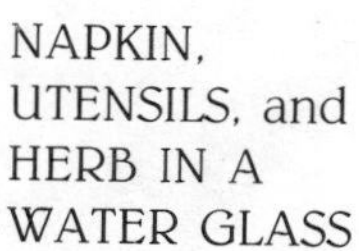

NAPKIN, UTENSILS, and HERB IN A WATER GLASS

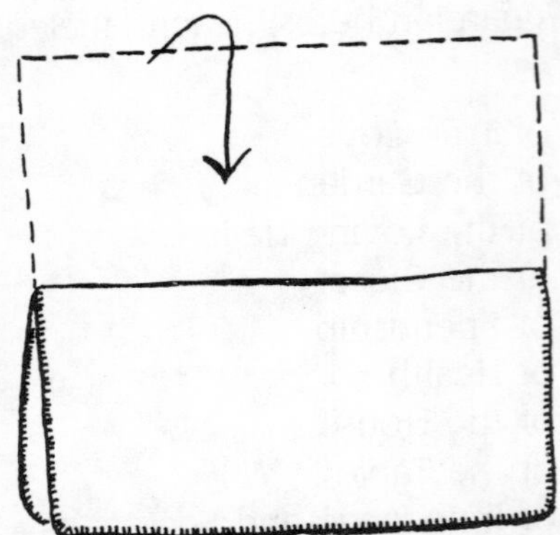

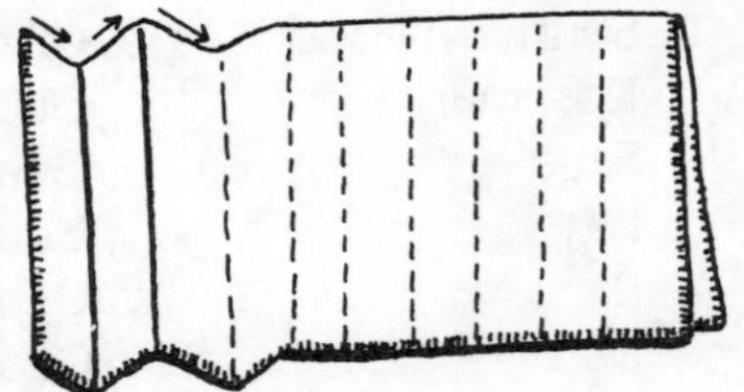

NOTHING IS MORE ELEGANT for any party than a display of crisp flaring linen napkins, folded and served in tall goblets, bistro style. Tuck in a sprig of herb or a small flower, kept fresh in a small florist tube of water.

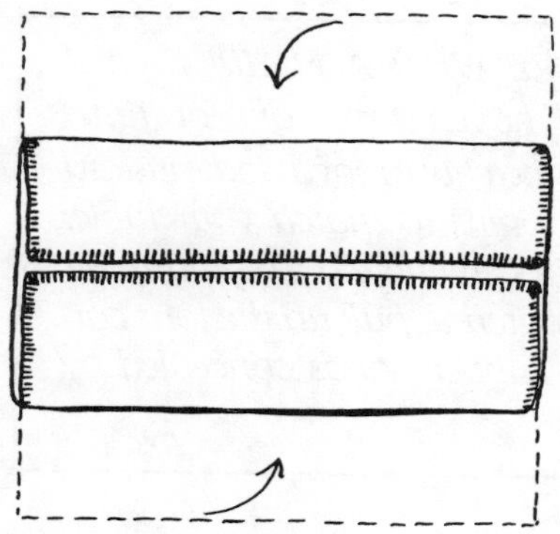

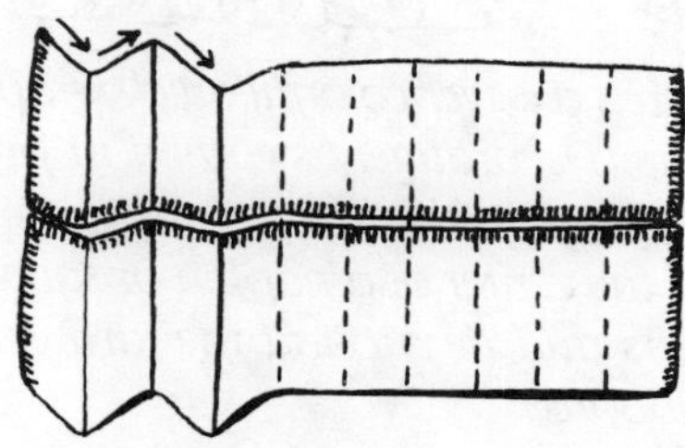

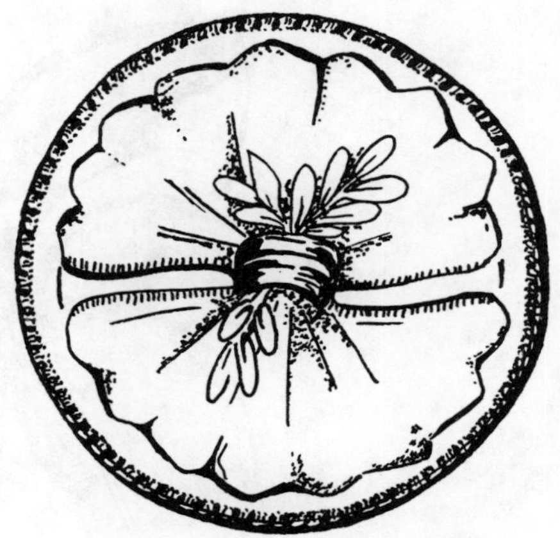

In Tudor times, sprigs of gilded rosemary were used at weddings. Gold spray makes this tradition easy to do. It will also serve to preserve the rosemary. Tuck gilded rosemary in your napkins.

Love note *SERVE WITH A FLAIR! Even if you haven't run out of time, here's a clever colorful quick wrap-up for ketchup, mayo and mustard jars. Decoratively swathed in pretty napkins to match your table, they are wisked from pantry to table in a twinkling. Place any jar in the center of a napkin or square of material, pull up the four corners and tie around the jar neck with rubber bands concealed by ribbons.*

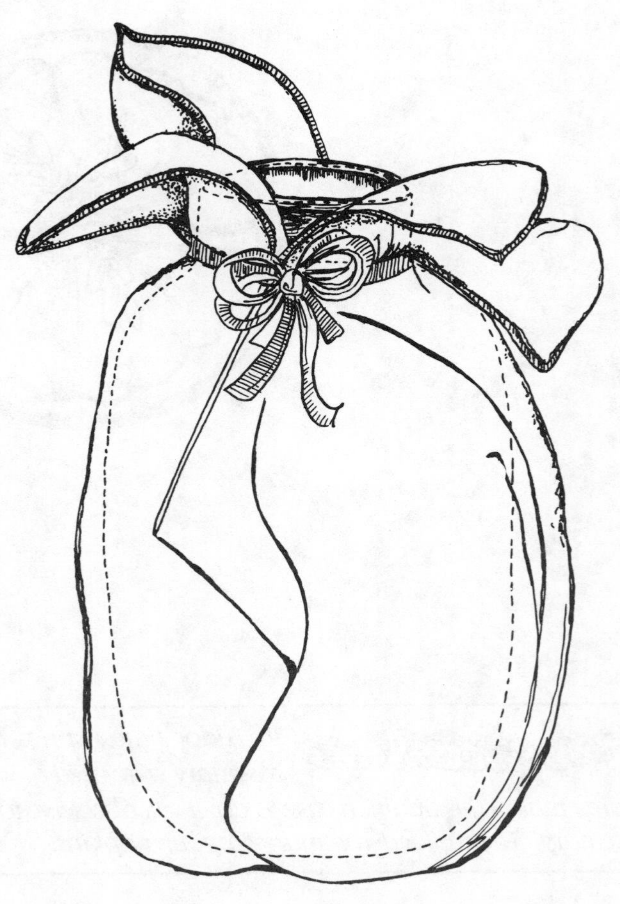

BUFFET DISHES
Main and Side

SUPERB MAIN COURSE CHICKEN SALAD

Stew your chicken(s) a day or two before the party. Cook them with celery, parsley, a touch of onion, bit of tarragon, a hint of rosemary and any other favorite seasonings. Cook, cool, bone and chunk the chicken. Reserve the broth for other use.

Using equal parts of chicken (4 cups) to finely minced celery (4 cups), combine with as much Hellman's Real Mayonnaise as necessary (4 cups). Serves 12

To this basic chicken salad, add any of the following (one or more, your choice)

black olives
diced red apple
green peas
chunked pineapple
hard boiled eggs
slivered almonds
other nuts
green grapes
avocado pieces
Mandarin oranges
pimiento
green pepper
red rose petals
water chestnuts

If the season permits, consider serving this delicious chicken salad in tulip cups or day lily blossoms as a substitute to lettuce.

TUNA MOUSSE

1 (13-oz.) can waterpacked solid white tuna
1 (8-oz.) pkg. cream cheese
1 can tomato soup (no water added)
2 envelopes plain gelatin dissolved in 1/2 cup cold water, then heated on low
3/4 C. finely chopped celery
3/4 C. chopped scallion and red onion mixture
2 heaping T. white horseradish
1 tsp. Worcestershire sauce
1 C. mayonnaise
Pepper and Tabasco to taste

Heat soup. Add cheese in small pieces and mix well (with wisk) until dissolved. Add gelatin, mix in well and take off the burner. Add tuna (completely minced and drained) and every-thing else. Mix well. Pour into lightly buttered mold. Takes a few hours to harden. Use a pretty mold and this will crown your party.

TOMATO-ROSE HIP ASPIC

(6-cup mold, dipped in cold water)
3 envelopes unflavored gelatin
2½ C. tomato juice, divided
1/2 C. rose hips
3 C. water
1 T. lemon juice
Lettuce (for garnish)

Soften the gelatin in 1 cup of tomato juice for 5 minutes.

Combine the rose hips and water in saucepan. Bring to a boil and simmer gently for 15 minutes. Strain, discarding the rose hips, and return the liquid to the saucepan. Add the softened gelatin.

Place over low heat, stirring until gelatin is dissolved. Add the lemon juice. Mix well. Turn into the prepared mold and chill until set. Unmold by dipping the mold into warm water.

Up to 1 cup of chopped vegetables may be added to the aspic. Before turning mixture into prepared mold, chill the mixture until slightly thickened, stirring occasionally. Stir in the chopped vegetables. Turn into the mold and chill until set. Garnish with real roses.

APRICOT SALAD MOLD

2 pkgs. apricot jello
3¾ C. boiling water
2 bananas, sliced thin
1 med. can crushed pineapple, drained, save juice
Topping:
1/2 C. sugar
1 egg
2 T. flour
1 T. butter
1/2 C. pineapple juice
1 pkg. Dream Whip
1 (3 oz.) pkg. cream cheese

Mix jello and water and put in 9x13" pan. Let soft set. Add bananas and pineapple. Cook topping — sugar, egg, flour, butter and juice — over medium heat until thickened. Add cream cheese, blend and cool. Make Dream Whip as directed on pkg. and add to topping. Spread on jello and fruit salad. Serves 15.

ITALIAN WEDDING SOUP

Into a large pot — 7 or 8-quart size — place a 3 lb. frying chicken and 6 quarts of water, 1 small bay leaf and 1 small onion. Cook 45 to 60 minutes until meat is soft, skimming off scum as chicken cooks. Remove chicken and let cool; debone and shred.

Meanwhile, add to soup, 3 celery stalks, chopped, and tiny meatballs made as follows:

3/4 to 1 lb. ground beef
1 egg
1/2 C. bread crumbs
3 T. grated cheese (Romano or Parmesan)
1 tsp. salt
1/8 tsp. black pepper
Dash of garlic powder
Chopped parsley, optional

Combine ingredients and add enough milk to form tiny meatballs the size of marbles.

Add meatballs to soup. Let cook and again remove any scum that appears. Then add 1½ lbs. of escarole or endive that has been thoroughly washed and drained and cut up. The chicken that has been shredded can be returned to the soup at this point.

Finally, add flour, dash of salt and 1 tsp. cheese to one beaten egg. Make into a thin paste and drizzle over the boiling soup. Paste should be consistency of pancake batter. Add a little water or milk to paste to get it to drizzle into soup.

FRUITED TURKEY SALAD

3 C. cubed cooked turkey
3/4 C. chopped celery
3/4 C. halved red grapes, seeded
1 (20-oz.) can pineapple chunks, drained
1 (11-oz.) can Mandarin oranges, drained
1/4 C. chopped pecans
1/4 C. salad dressing
1/8 tsp. salt

Combine all ingredients and chill well before serving. Serve in lettuce cups. Makes 6 servings.

PRETTY PARTY SANDWICH LOAF

1 C. butter or margarine softened
1 C. (1/4 lb.) grated American cheese
1 C. (1/4 lb.) grated Port Salut cheese
1 (8 oz.) pkg. cream cheese
2 oz. Bleu cheese
2 tsp. paprika
1 tsp. Worcestershire sauce
1/2 C. dairy sour cream
1/2 C. chopped, pimiento-stuffed olives
4 hard-boiled eggs, chopped
1 tsp. curry powder
2 cans (41/2 oz.) deviled ham
1/4 C. heavy cream
3-lb. Pullman loaf of bread, unsliced
pimiento strips
Whole pimiento-stuffed olives

Combine 1/2 cup of the butter with cheeses, paprika, Worcestershire sauce and sour cream; beat until well blended. Take out 1½ cups cheese mixture and stir in chopped olives; reserve for filling. Mix together chopped eggs, remaining 1/2 cup butter and curry powder; reserve for filling. Mix deviled ham with heavy cream; reserve for filling.

Remove crusts from Pullman loaf; slice bread lengthwise into 4 long slices. Spread ham filling on bottom layer of bread, top with second layer and spread with olive-cheese filling. Top with third layer and spread with egg filling. Top with fourth layer and frost entire loaf with remaining cheese mixture. Run tines of fork along loaf for bark-like appearance. Decorate top of loaf with strips of pimiento and whole olives. Chill several hours or over-night. Slice with sharp knife to serve. Makes 16" loaf.

SHARON'S EASY AND DELICIOUS HAM CASSEROLE

2 C. dry macaroni
2 C. evaporated milk
2 C. grated cheese (cheddar/sharp)
1½ C. ham cubes
2 cans Cream of Golden Mushroom soup
1 med. onion, diced

Mix all the above in a bowl. Pour into greased casserole dish. Bake 1 hour at 350°

(Optional: Add 3 hard boiled eggs, diced during the last 10 min. of baking time.)

SUPERBOWL COLESLAW

(from Heloise)

FIRST: Hardcook two eggs, peel and soak in red beet juice until the whites turn a gorgeous color. (These can be purchased at some delicatessens.) Grate or chop the eggs.

SECOND: Cut cabbage head in half and soak in salty ice water several hours. Shake off excess water and cut in half again. Shred as thinly as possible.

THIRD: Combine eggs and cut up cabbage.

FOURTH: Mix up this dressing, toss, and refrigerate:

2 oz. vegetable oil
1 oz. lemon juice
1/2 tsp. prepared mustard
Dash of paprika
1/4 tsp. celery salt
1 oz. mayonnaise
Salt to taste
Freshly ground pepper

SALAD BANANA SPLITS

Ham salad (with minced parsley)
Chicken salad (with minced celery)
Cottage cheese (with minced chives)
1/2 banana for each guest
Red cherries
Green olives
Black olives

Serve this decorative luncheon dish proudly. Easily assembled, it is most attractive. Purchase long disposable sundae dishes and place a long sliced half banana in each. Top it with a scoop of ham salad and another scoop of chicken salad on each side of a scoop of cottage cheese. Top each with a garnish of chopped or minced herbs, cherries and olives to simulate a banana split. Serve with deviled egg, a kiwi slice, pickled beet and a roll. A simple dessert and beverage completes this fun menu.

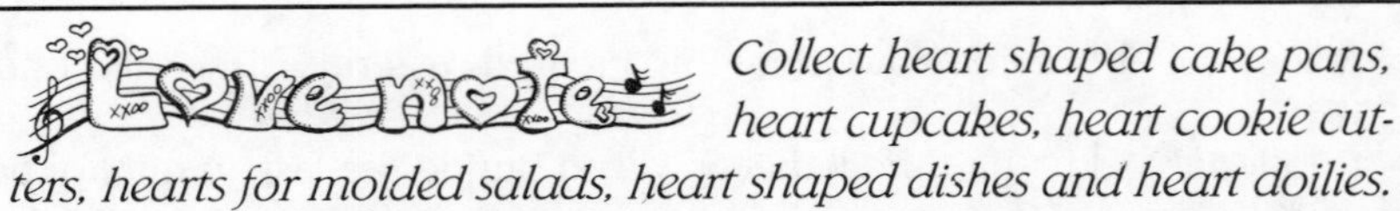

Collect heart shaped cake pans, heart cupcakes, heart cookie cutters, hearts for molded salads, heart shaped dishes and heart doilies.

IMPOSSIBLE HAM 'n' SWISS PIE

2 C. cut-up, fully cooked, smoked ham
1 C. shredded natural Swiss cheese (about 4 oz.)
1/3 C. chopped green onions or chopped onion
4 eggs
2 C. milk
1 C. Bisquick baking mix
1/4 tsp. salt, if desired
1/8 tsp. pepper

Heat oven to 400°. Grease pie plate, 10x11/2". Sprinkle ham, cheese and onions in plate. Beat remaining ingredients until smooth, 15 seconds in blender on high or 1 min. with hand beater. Pour into plate. Bake until golden brown and knife inserted in center comes out clean, 35 to 40 min. Cool 5 min. Makes 6 servings.

THREE-CHEESE BROCCOLI BAKE

1 C. Bisquick baking mix
1/4 C. finely chopped onion
1/4 C. milk
2 eggs
1/2 C. grated Parmesan cheese
1 carton (12 oz.) creamed cottage cheese
1 (10. oz) pkg. frozen chopped broccoli, thawed and drained
4 oz. Monterey Jack cheese, cut into 1/2" cubes
2 cloves garlic, crushed
2 eggs

Heat oven to 375°. Grease rectangular baking dish, 12x7½x2". Mix baking mix, oninon, milk and 2 eggs; beat vigorously 20 strokes. Spread in dish. Mix remaining ingredients; spoon evenly over batter in dish. Bake until set, about 30 min. Cool 5 min. Makes 6 to 8 servings.

LEMON-MINT RICE

1 C. rice
1/4 C. butter or margarine
1 tsp. finely chopped parsley
1/4 tsp. each grated lemon peel and dried mint

Cook rice according to package directions. Toss with butter, parsley, lemon peel and dried mint. Makes 4 servings.

Love note

Entice your guests with a menu of "stratified" foods, such as Cheese Strata, Fruit Strata, and Salad Strata. The recipes are easily prepared twenty-four hours in advance, allowing you the freedom to enjoy your party and your guests. Just add some crackers to go with the salad, cookies to go with the fruit and have a hot or cold beverage. Your reputation as a hostess is assured with these delicious and gorgeous recipes.

SWISS CHEESE STRATA

1 loaf French bread, cut into 1-inch cubes (about 8 c.)
1 can (11 oz.) condensed Cheddar cheese soup
2 C. shredded Swiss cheese
4 eggs, slightly beaten
1 soup can water
1 T. oregano
1/3 C. sauterne or other dry white wine

In buttered 2-qt. shallow baking dish (12x8x2"), arrange bread cubes. In bowl, combine remaining ingredients; pour over bread. Cover: refrigerate 6 hours or over-night. Uncover; bake at 350° for 30 min. or until hot. Makes 6-8 servings.

FRUIT STRATA

1 C. melon balls or cubes
1 C. blueberries
1 C. peach slices
1 C. strawberries or raspberries
1/2 C. lowfat pineapple yogurt
Mint sprigs, pineapple sage, lemon verbena and/or rose geranium leaves

Layer colorful fresh fruits in a large glass bowl (my favorite is a tall stemmed compote). Lay down a few herbs and spread yogurt on top. Cover and chill for at least two hours (can be made 24 hours in advance). Garnish with additional berries and the rest of the herbs (kept fresh in a glass of water in the refrigerator). Makes 6-8 servings.

SALAD STRATA

1 head lettuce
Several stalks celery
2 green peppers
1 sweet onion
1 (10 oz.) box frozen peas
1 C. sour cream
1 C. mayonnaise
2 T. sugar
1/4 lb. cheddar cheese
1 C. herbs: parsley, mint, chervil, burnet, lovage, etc., all minced

Quarter, wash, drain, cut fine and pat dry lettuce. Wash and scrape celery, cut into small pieces (about 2 cups). Wash, core, cut in strips green peppers; cut onions into thin rings or chop. Cook peas (no butter) in a little salted water. Drain. Place in layers in glass bowl in order given, saving 1/2 of lettuce as top layer. Mix sour cream and mayonnaise together and spread over salad. Do not stir. Sprinkle 2 T. sugar over salad and cover all with grated cheddar cheese. Cover bowl with plastic. Refrigerate 24 hours or at least 8 hours after which it emerges cold and crisp. Serves 8 generously.

TOASTED SESAME SALAD

1/2 C. sesame seeds
1 T. butter
1/4 C. grated Parmesan cheese
1 C. dairy sour cream
1/2 C. mayonnaise
1 T. tarragon vinegar
1 T. sugar
1 tsp. salt
clove garlic, minced
2 heads Bibb or leaf lettuce
1 cucumber, thinly sliced
1/2 green pepper, chopped
2 green onions, sliced
1 carrot, pared, cut in thin strips

In small skillet saute seeds in butter until lightly browned. Remove from heat and add Parmesan cheese. Set aside. In small bowl blend sour cream with mayonnaise. Add vinegar, sugar, salt and garlic. Tear lettuce into bite size pieces in salad bowl. Add cucumber, pepper, onions and carrots. Toss with 1/2 of sesame seed mixture. Sprinkle remaining seeds on top. If desired, garnish with tomato slices or wedges. Serves 6-9.

WEDDING and PARTY CAKES

The Wedding Cake is another object of romantic history. A ring is sometimes baked into the cake and the person who finds it is supposed to be the next one to marry. Also, small pieces of the cake are regularly distributed to be taken home and placed under the pillow, it being presumed that one's future husband will thus reveal himself in a dream.

The cake itself has had quite a long and interesting history. At the Roman confarreatio, a form of marriage, the couple ate a cake made of salt, water, and flour. The bride carried three wheat ears as a symbol of plenty or fruitfulness. In the Middle Ages this custom took the form of throwing wheat grains after the bride, and later, of baking the grains into biscuits which were broken over the bride's head. Still later it became the custom in England to bring small richly spiced buns to a wedding. These were piled into a tall mound over which the bride and groom were to kiss. If they succeeded, prosperity was assured them. But the mounds were cumbersome, and it is said, a French cook conceived the idea of icing them into a solid whole. This, then, was the origin of the wedding cake. Traditionally the bride herself cuts the first slice as a security that no outside force shall cut into her happiness.

taken from The Book of Knowledge

MINGA'S WEDDING CAKE

This memorable wedding, which featured garden flowers galore, was crowned with the best cake I've ever eaten. If you don't want to make it yourself, assemble all the ingredients and take it to your best local baker. It's worth any effort.

Bride's Cake

8 egg whites
(Reserve yolks for groom's cake.)
2 C. sugar
1 C. butter
1 C. light cream
3½ C. flour
4 tsp. baking powder
1/2 lb. chopped almonds
1/2 lb. grated coconut
1/4 lb. candied orange peel, finely chopped
1 tsp. lemon extract
1 tsp. vanilla

Beat egg whites until stiff. Beat in 1 C. sugar, 2 T. at a time, and set aside. Cream butter and remaining cup of sugar. Add flavorings. Mix and sift dry ingredients and add alternately with the cream. Mix in fruit and nuts. Fold in beaten egg whites.

To cut round tiers, move in two inches from the tier's outer edge; cut a circle and then slice 1-in. pieces within the circle. Now move in another 2-in., cut another circle, slice 1-in. pieces and so on until the tier is completely cut. The center core of each tier and the small top tier can be cut into halves, 4ths, 6ths and 8ths, depending on size.

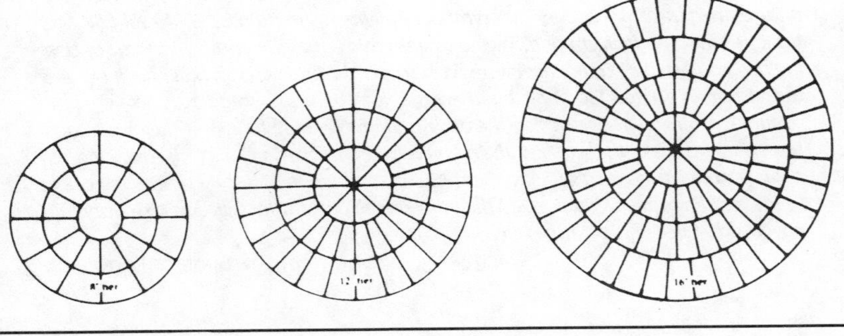

Groom's Cake

1/2 C. sugar
1½ C. brown sugar
1 C. butter
8 egg yolks
3 C. flour
1 lb. seeded raisins
1/2 lb. dried currants
1/4 lb. candied orange peel, finely chopped
1/4 lb. chopped nuts
1 C. whiskey
1 tsp. soda
Generous 1/2 tsp. each of cloves, nutmeg, cinnamon, allspice.

Cream sugars and butter, then add egg yolks and beat well. Add flour mixed with soda and spices alternately with whiskey. Mix in fruit and nuts.

For each cake, butter and flour three pans; 12, 9 and 6 inches in diameter. Bake in a slow oven 300-325° for 1 to 1½ hours depending on pan size. Cool in pans 10 minutes, then remove from pans and put on cake racks to cool completely. May be stored for several days wrapped separately in foil and may also be frozen. When ready to use, put together in graduated layers with Minga's Wedding Cake Icing.

MINGA'S WEDDING CAKE ICING

1 C. soft butter
6 lbs. sifted confectioner's sugar
1/2 tsp. salt
8-10 egg whites
1/2 C. light cream
3 tsp. vanilla

In a large bowl cream and beat butter till light. Add salt and vanilla and mix in. Gradually add sugar and egg whites alter-nately and beat well. Add enough cream for a good spreading consistency. Do not tint Wedding Cake Icing. Icing is easier made in two batches.

Cover a round piece of white cardboard with a large lace paper doily. Protect this with strips of waxed paper which may be pulled out when finished decorating. Place the 12-inch Groom's Cake on this, frost thinly and top with the 12-inch Bride's Cake. Cut a 9-inch round of white cardboard and center on the lower cakes. Place 9-inch Groom's Cake on this, frost thinly and top with 9-inch Bride's Cake. Do the same with the 6-inch layers. Now frost the whole cake. Pipe rosettes of icing around edges of each layer. Place a small nosegay of fresh flowers in the center of the 6-inch layer.

To cut: Cut first layer all the way around, then the second layer around. First layer around again. Save the top for the Bride. Then cut rest of cake. (See diagram)

HAVE A BIG HEART

If you do not have heart shaped cake pans, a large romantic party cake is easily made from a square and a round pan, 8" or 9" or larger. Cut the round one in half and place as shown. Decorate with fresh flowers and herbs or with icing.

Of course, a larger more impressive heart is made from a larger square and round pans. Place them on wooden boards, cut to size and cover with foil. Make several large heart cakes for a large crowd for a dramatic table setting that sets the scene for any bridal party.

These cakes can be made from any favorite family recipe or use a box cake mix.

NANCY'S CARROT WEDDING CAKE

1½ C. vegetable oil
1½ C. sugar
4 eggs, well beaten
3 C. grated carrots
2 C. unbleached flour
1/2 tsp. salt
2 tsp. soda
2 tsp. cinnamon
2 tsp. allspice
(or 1 T. apple pie spice)
1 C. chopped pecans
1 C. raisins
1 tsp. vanilla

Cream the oil and sugar then add eggs and carrots. Mix well. Mix together dried ingredients and add to the carrot mixture, a small amount at a time, beating well. Then add nuts, raisins and vanilla. Pour into 9x13" greased and sugared pan and bake 1 hour at 325°. Cool before frosting.

Frosting

1/2 C. butter at room temperature
1 (8 oz.) pkg. cream cheese, softened
4 C. powder sugar
1 tsp. vanilla
1 C. chopped nuts (add or sprinkled on top)

Cream the butter and cheese. Add sugar and vanilla and beat. Frost. Keep cake refrigerated but serve at room temperature.

MEXICAN WEDDING CAKE

1 C. chopped pecans
1 (20 oz.) can crushed pineapple, undrained
2 C. sugar
2 C. flour
1 tsp. baking soda
1/2 tsp. salt
2 tsp. vanilla
2 eggs

Combine all ingredients in a large bowl and mix well. Pour into a greased and floured 9"x13" pan. Bake 45 to 50 minutes at 350°. Serves 12-15.

Icing

1 (8 oz.) pkg. cream cheese
1/2 C. margarine
1½ C. powdered sugar
2 tsp. vanilla

Mix together and spread on cooled cake.

COOL AND MINTY BRIDAL CAKE

1 (14 oz.) can Eagle Brand Sweetened Condensed Milk (not evaporated milk)
2 tsp. peppermint extract
8 drops green food coloring
2 C. (1 pint) whipping cream, whipped *(do not use non-dairy whipped topping)*
1 (18½-oz.) pkg. white cake mix
Green creme de menthe
1 (8-oz.) container frozen non-dairy whipped topping, thawed

In large bowl, mix sweetened condensed milk, extract and food coloring. Fold in whipped cream.

Pour into aluminum foil-lined 9-inch round layer cake pan. Cover. Freeze 6 hours or until firm.

Meanwhile, prepare and bake cake mix as package directs for two 9-inch round layers. Remove from pan; cool completely.

With table fork, poke holes in layers 1 inch apart halfway through each layer. Drizzle small amounts of creme de menthe in holes.

Place cake layer on serving plate; top with ice cream layer then second cake layer. Frost with non-dairy whipped topping. (Makes one 9-inch cake)

ITALIAN LOVE CAKE

1 angel food cake
1/2 C. amaretto
1 pint pistachio ice cream
1 pint strawberry ice cream
2 C. (1/2 pint) heavy cream
1 (6 oz.) pkg. semisweet chocolate morsels

With a sharp serrated knife, using a sawing motion, cut the cake into three layers. Sprinkle layers with 6 T. of the amaretto. Place one layer on a serving platter. Cut ice cream into slices and place pistachio ice cream on bottom layer. Top with second cake layer and a layer of strawberry ice cream. Top with third cake layer. Place in freezer. In a bowl, mix heavy cream and remaining amaretto and beat until very thick. Frost the sides and top of the cake and replace in freezer. Melt chocolate over very low heat until smooth. Spread chocolate in a 1/4-inch thick layer on foil and chill until chocolate hardens. With a small cookie cutter, cut hearts out of chocolate and place on top of cake. Freeze cake until ready to serve. Makes a 9-inch cake.

LIME-MINT SHERBET

12 sprigs fresh mint
2 C. water
3/4 C. sugar
1/2 C. light corn syrup
2 tsp. grated lime rind
1/2 C. lime juice
Green food coloring
2 egg whites, stiffly beaten

Set freezer control for fast freezing. Pick mint leaves from stems and chop. Add water and sugar. Bring to a boil, stirring until the sugar dissolves. Cool and strain. Add corn syrup, lime rind and juice; tint with coloring. Freeze until firm. Break up mixture and beat until it is a smooth mush. Fold in the egg whites and freeze until firm. Yield: 2 pints.

MELISSA'S LEMON JELLO

Make a tea of lemon balm leaves steeped in boiling water (see Lemon Balm Jelly) for ten mintues. Use the strained liquid to make lemon jello. Capture a sweet woodruff whorled leaf on top.

Be aware of dieting friends and serve low calorie foods attractively and creatively. Sugar free jello sparkles like a jewel when served in tall wine glasses.

SPICED ICED ORANGES

16 Amaretto cookies
8 large oranges, peeled
1/4 tsp. cinnamon, ground
1/2 tsp. cloves, ground
1/3 C. sugar
1 C. orange liqueur
Sprigs of mint

Crush cookies. Slice oranges thinly, toss with spices and freeze. Add the juice to liqueur and reserve. To serve oranges, pile frozen segments in elegant stemmed glasses. Sprinkle with liqueur, top with crushed cookies, garnish with mint and serve.

SPICY GINGERBREAD

3/4 C. Crisco
3/4 C. packed brown sugar
2 eggs
3/4 C. dark molasses
2½ C. flour
2 tsp. baking powder
2 tsp. ground ginger
1 tsp. black pepper
1½ tsp. cinnamon
1/2 tsp. ground cloves
1/2 tsp. nutmeg
1/2 tsp. baking soda
1/2 tsp. salt
1 C. boiling water

Cream shortening and brown sugar. Add eggs, beating after each one. Add molasses and mix well. Stir all dry ingredients together with a wire whisk. Add dry mixture alternately with water to the molasses mixture. Pour mixture into well-greased and floured 9-inch pan. Bake at 350° for 45-50 minutes until center springs back when touched with fingertip. Serve warm or cold. Tangy Lemon Sauce is delicious on it.

TANGY LEMON SAUCE

1 C. sugar
3 T. cornstarch
2 C. water
1 T. grated lemon peel
2 egg yolks, beaten
2 T. soft butter
1½ C. lemon juice

Combine sugar and cornstarch in pan; gradually add water, blending until smooth. Cook over medium heat, stirring con-stantly till mixture becomes thick and clear. Remove from heat. Stir small amount of hot mixture into egg yolks and then add egg yolks to the hot mixture in the saucepan and cook 2 minutes. Add lemon juice, lemon peel and butter. Blend well. Serve warm or cool. Makes 2¾ cups.

Instead of Lemon Sauce, grind 3 T. sweet cicely leaves and 1 C. powdered sugar in a mortar with pestle. Dust it through a paper doily for a lacey pattern on your gingerbread.

QUICK-AND-EASY POPPY SEED CAKE

1/2 C. poppy seed
1-1/3 C. water
1 pkg. white cake mix
1 can prepared vanilla pudding
1 pkg. fluffy white frosting mix

Soak poppy seed in water at least 1 hour. Bake cake in 2 round layer pans, 8" or 9", as directed on package except substitute poppy seed mixture for water. Cool. Fill layers with 1 C. of pudding; spread remaining pudding on top. Prepare frosting as directed on package; frost side and top of cake. Refrigerate leftover cake.

HAWAIIAN WEDDING CAKE

1 box yellow cake mix

Bake cake according to package directions in a 13x9 inch pan. Let cool.

1 C. milk
1 box instant vanilla pudding
1 (8-oz.) pkg. cream cheese

Mix all ingredients and spread over cooled cake.

Drain: One 20-oz. can crushed pineapple. Spread over pudding mixture.

Next: Smooth over pineapple, 1 large pkg. whipped topping, prepared as directed.

Last: Sprinkle over top 1 can flaked coconut. Refrigerate until serving time.
This is exquisite on a lie of lemon balm.

COOKIES

MATRIMONIAL BARS

1¾ C. flour
1/2 tsp. baking soda
3/4 C. butter or margarine, softened
1 C. packed brown sugar
1½ C. quick oats
1 (12 oz.) jar strawberry or raspberry jam (1 C.)

Stir together flour and soda; set aside. In medium bowl, cream butter and sugar until light and fluffy. Stir in flour mixture until well blended. Blend in oats (with fingers or wooden spoon). Dough will be crumbly. Press half the dough into greased 13x9-inch pan. Spread with jam. Crumble remaining dough over top; pat lightly to cover. Bake in preheated 400° oven 20 to 25 min. or until lightly browned. While warm, cut in 2x11/2-inch bars and remove from pan. Serve warm or cooled. Store airtight in cool place. Makes 30.

CRISP CARAWAY COOKIES

1⅔ C. flour
1 tsp. baking powder
1/4 tsp. baking soda
1/4 tsp. salt
2 tsp. caraway seed
1/2 C. butter or margarine, softened
2/3 C. sugar
2 eggs
1/2 tsp. vanilla

Mix flour, baking powder, soda, salt and caraway seed; set aside. Cream butter and sugar until fluffy. Add eggs and vanilla; beat well. Stir in flour mixture. Wrap dough in plastic wrap and chill several hours or overnight or until firm enough to roll (dough will still be rather soft). Working with one fourth of the dough at a time (keep remainder refrigerated), roll very thin on floured surface (easiest with pastry cloth and rolling-pin cover). Cut with floured 3-inch round cutter. Put on ungreased cookie sheets. Bake on top rack of preheated 375° oven 8 to 10 minutes, watching closely. Remove to rack to cool. Repeat. Store airtight or freeze. Makes about 48.

MEXICAN WEDDING COOKIES

1 C. butter or margarine, softened
Confectioners' sugar
1 tsp. pure vanilla
1/4 tsp. salt
2 C. flour

In medium bowl, cream butter, 1/2 C. sugar, vanilla and salt until fluffy. Stir in flour until well blended. Chill 30 minutes or until firm enough to handle. Shape in 1-inch balls. Place 1 inch apart on ungreased cookie sheet; bake in preheated 375° oven 12 to 15 minutes or until lightly golden. Remove to rack (close together) and while still warm, dust heavily with confectioners' sugar; cool. Store airtight in cool dry place. Before serving, dust cookies with additional confectioners' sugar. Makes 48.

LEMON CARAWAY REFRIGERATOR COOKIES

2⅓ C. flour
1/2 tsp. baking soda
1/2 C. butter or margarine, softened
1 C. sugar
1 egg
2 T. lemon juice
1 tsp. grated lemon peel
1¼ tsp. caraway seed
Colored sugar (optional)

Stir together flour and baking soda; set aside. In medium bowl cream butter and sugar. Beat in egg until light and fluffy. Beat in lemon juice, peel and caraway seed until blended. Stir in flour mixture just until well blended. Shape in roll about 2 inches thick. Wrap; chill 1 hour. If roll is flat on bottom, roll on counter so cookies will be round when cut. Chill several hours more or overnight. With very sharp knife cut in 1/4-inch slices. Place on greased cookie sheets; sprinkle with colored sugar. Bake in preheated 375° oven 10 minutes or until lightly browned around the edges. Remove immediately to racks to cool. Store loosely covered in cool, dry place. Makes 36.

MELISSA'S LEMON WHIPPERSNAPS

1 pkg. lemon cake mix (18½ oz.)
1 egg
3 tsp. dried lemon balm
2 C. (4½ oz.) frozen whipped topping, thawed
1/2 C. sifted powdered sugar

Grease cookie sheets. Combine cake mix, whipped topping, lemon balm and egg in large bowl. Stir until well mixed. Drop by teaspoons into powdered sugar, roll to coat. Place 1½ inches apart on cookie sheet. Bake at 350° for 10 to 15 min. until light golden brown. Remove from cookie sheet. Cool. Makes about 4 doz. cookies.

ENGLISH TASSIES

Filling:
3/4 to 1 C. chopped pecans (reserve 1/4 C. for top)
2 T. melted butter
2 eggs
pinch of salt
1½ C. light brown sugar
a few drops of vanilla

Shells:
1/4 lb. butter
1 C. sifted flour
1 small pkg. cream cheese

Cream together butter and cream cheese; add sifted flour. Put in refrigerator to chill as it will handle better. Divide into balls (20-25 or more). Press into small muffin tins to form shells. Mix together filling ingredients; beat until blended. Fill the shells and sprinkle nuts on top. Bake at 350° for 35 minutes. Take out of pans while slightly warm.

ENGLISH TARTS

Filling:
2 C. sugar
1 lb. raisins
1 C. butter
4 eggs, beaten
1 C. chopped nuts
1 tsp. cinnamon

Pastry:
1¼ C. flour
1/3 C. plus 1 T. shortening
1/4 tsp. salt
3-4 T. milk

Cook filling until thickened, stirring to prevent scorching. Cool. Mix pastry with blender. Roll out and cut. Place pastry circles in smallest muffin tins, fill with filling. Bake 15 min. at 400°. Reduce to 350° and bake till crust is brown — about 15-20 min.

FRUIT IS ALWAYS FESTIVE

MINT DRESSING FOR FRUIT

1/2 C. sugar
1½ C. salad oil
1 C. lemon juice
1½ tsp. salt
1/2 tsp. mint extract or
1 8-inch long sprig fresh mint leaves*

EARLY IN DAY OR UP TO 1 MONTH AHEAD:

Into covered blender container, place sugar, salad oil, lemon juice, salt and mint extract; blend at medium speed until mixture is smooth. Pour dressing into 1-quart bottle or container; cover and refrigerate. Shake before using on fruit salad. Makes 31/2 cups.

* If using mint leaves, place leaves in bottle or container first. In covered blender container, blend sugar, salad oil, lemon juice and salt until mixture is smooth; pour into bottle; cover and refrigerate at least 12 hours for flavor to develop. Serve as above.

FRUIT SALAD DRESSING #1

1 (6 oz.) can frozen lemonade concentrate, thawed
1 (6 oz.) can frozen orange juice concentrate, thawed
1 C. salad oil
1 T. honey
1/2 T. Worcestershire sauce
Dash of cayenne pepper
6 T. finely diced candied ginger

Blend all ingredients except ginger in blender (or shake vigorously in a tightly covered jar). Add ginger. Keeps well refrigerated. Shake before serving. Makes 2 cups.

MELISSA'S AMBROSIA

6 large sweet navel oranges
1 large can pineapple slices, drained
1 small can flaked coconut
1/4 C. sugar
1/2 C. lemon balm leaves
2/3 C. sweet sherry

Peel, thinly slice cross-wise and seed oranges. Arrange 3 oranges in a large shallow dessert bowl. Alternate with half the pineapple slices, sprinkle with half the coconut, lemon balm and sugar. Repeat this using remaining ingredients. Pour the sherry evenly over all. Cover bowl with plastic wrap and chill until serving time. Serves 6 to 8.

FRUIT SALAD DRESSING #2

1 C. orange juice
6 T. honey
4 T. chopped sweet cicely leaves

Simmer 2 minutes to blend. Pour over fruits in salad and chill before serving.

WEDDING FRUIT SALAD

1 (1 lb. 4 oz.) can pineapple chunks in own juice, well-drained
2 bananas, peeled and thinly sliced
2 oranges, peeled and sectioned
3 kiwis, peeled and thinly sliced
1 pt. strawberries, washed and hulled
1 C. melon balls
1 T. lemon verbene leaves, chopped
Lettuce leaves, optional

DRESSING

1 clove garlic, peeled and crushed slightly
5 T. lemon juice
1 C. cranberry juice cocktail
1 T. light corn syrup or honey
1/2 tsp. salt
1/4 tsp. paprika

To prepare dressing: Let garlic stand in lemon juice at room temperature for at least 2 hours; remove. Add remaining ingredients; blend well. Chill. Shake well before pouring over prepared fruit. Arrange pineapple chunks, banana slices, orange sections, kiwi slices, whole strawberries and melon balls in lettuce lined salad bowl.

SKEWERS OF BEAUTIFUL FRUITS

Using 8" bamboo skewers, available at any kitchen shop, line up chunks of pineapple, green grapes, Maraschino cherries, a mushroom, square of cheese, thick slice of banana (rolled in lemon juice to keep from browning) and a segment of Mandarin orange. This pretty array is both side dish and/or garnish.

FRUIT CLOUD

A picture perfect fruit dessert to steal the show.

Step 1:

2 egg whites, at room temperature
1/2 T. cream of tartar
1/8 tsp. salt
1/4 tsp. vanilla
2/3 C. sugar

Beat all but sugar until the mixture holds its peaks. Slowly add sugar while continuing to beat until stiff and glossy.

On greased brown paper on a cooky sheet, make an 8-inch meringue shell with a bottom crust 1/4 inch thick and sides about 2 inches high. Bake in slow oven (275°) 1 hour or till crisp and cream-colored. Cool; remove to a flat dish.

Step 2:

1/2 C. heavy cream
1 T. powdered sugar

Whip cream and sugar then spread in bottom in meringue shell.

Step 3:

1 pkg. lemon chiffon pie filling prepared according to box directions.

One hour before serving time, add 1½ C. fruits of your choice, cut small for pie filling. Pour fruit mixture over cream in meringue shell.

Step 4:

At serving time, top with more fruit and whipped cream. Serves 8. Garnish with sprigs of lemon balm and lemon verbena.

KATY'S BLUEBERRY SOUP

Boil 1 C. water with 1/2 C. sugar and 1 cinnamon stick, until sugar is dissolved. Mix 2 T. cornstarch with 1/4 C. water and add to boiling mixture. Boil until clear. Remove from heat and add: 1 (6 oz.) can frozen lemonade concentrate, 1 qt. buttermilk, 1 qt. blueberries (smash some of the blueberries so they release their color). Blend in 1 small carton of blueberry yogurt. Stir soup with the cinnamon stick or remove the stick before serving. Top with a dollop of whipped cream and a sprig of mint.

Recipe from Katy's Kitchen.

SUMMER DESSERT PLATTER

1/4 watermelon, sliced in one-inch pieces
1 lb. pineapple spears (fresh) or chunks (unsweetened, canned)
3 large oranges, peeled, sliced into rounds
1 pt. strawberries, washed, hulled
4 medium peaches, pared, sliced, dipped into lemon juice
1 pt. blueberries, washed
1 lb. seedless grapes, washed, divided into small bunches
1 lb. red grapes, washed, divided into small bunches
4 medium bananas, peeled, cut into rounds, dipped into lemon juice
1 pt. lime sherbet

Arrange the watermelon wedges in the center of a large platter, around a glass dish (to hold sherbet). Select four or more of the suggested fruits; prepare them, and arrange them in groups around the tray. Add the bananas and peaches (if used) just before serving; as well as placing the sherbet in the dish. Garnish lavishly with mint, lemon verbena, parsley, burnet, lovage and edible flowers. Serves six.

FABULOUS FRUIT COMPOTE

1 (1 lb. 1 oz.) can pitted dark, sweet cherries
1 (1 lb.) can sliced peaches, drained
1 (12 oz). pkg. dried apricots
1 T. grated orange peel
1 T. grated lemon peel
1/2 C. orange juice
1/4 C. lemon juice
1/2 tsp. ground cardamon
3/4 C. light-brown sugar, packed
Sour cream or sweetened whipped cream

Preheat oven to 350°. Turn cherries and their liquid into a 2-qt. casserole. Add peaches, apricots, orange and lemon peels and juices. Sprinkle with brown sugar.

Bake, covered, 11/2 hours. Let cool slightly; then refrigerate, covered, several hours or overnight, or until well chilled. Serve with sour cream or sweetened whipped cream. Serves 6 to 8.

GRAPES ROYALE

Two simple ingredients — sour cream and brown sugar — put this elegant dessert in the gourmet class.

Stir 1 C. dairy sour cream into 4 C. stemmed, washed, seedless grapes (about 2 pounds) in medium-size bowl; chill until serving time. Spoon into a serving bowl or individual dessert dishes; sprinkle lightly with 2 T. brown sugar. Garnish with mint. Makes 6 servings.

MINTED GRAPES

Green grapes in small bunches
2 egg whites, beaten frothy (can be colored green)
1 C. granulated sugar
2 peppermint tea bags

Wash and pat dry grapes. Dip in frothy egg whites. Place on waxed paper, cover completely with sugar mixed with dried peppermint tea. Allow to dry in refrigerator until serving time.

If you're planning a wedding party, make your guests who are waist watchers happy with food and drinks that are high in taste appeal, but low in calories, such as chicken breasts, enticing fruit salads, and diet drinks.

Sometimes it seems as though absolutely everybody is on a diet — a fact that can put a crimp in the menu planning of any hostess. You can't fight the diet craze, so join it by planning party menus with a light touch. Let "herbs make the difference."

THINGS TO DRINK WITH TOASTS

By those we love —
— May we be loved

HOT MULLED CIDER

Stick 6 oranges full of cloves Bake in oven until soft and juicy. Place in crock pot. Pour 2 gallons apple cider over oranges in crock pot. Then add:

1 tsp. ground cloves, cinnamon, allspice and/or ginger
1 tsp. freshly grated nutmeg

Stir with long cinnamon sticks. Keep heated while serving. Serve with short cinnamon sticks.

SIX SUGGESTED HERB TEAS

Peppermint

The number one herb tea that everyone loves. Symbolizing virtue, mint was considered so valuable, at one time it was used for tithing. It has a cool, mouth cleansing effect and is an aid to the digestion.

Hibiscus

This rosey-red drink has a taste that has a citrus-tart tang. Children are especially fond of this red thirst-quenching beverage. In Africa it is called "Carcadeeh," which means *Beverage that brings health.*

Rose Hip Blend

The rose, which symbolizes love, has been eaten for centuries. Rose water, rose wine and rose petal preserves are still enjoyed today. The seedpods of the rose, or rose hips, contain an enormous amount of valuable vitamin C. Rose Hips tea has a delectable, fruity, wine-like taste. It is especially good mixed with hibiscus tea.

Comfrey

Comfrey brews into a very light, delicately flavored beverage. The tea is composed of the dried leaves of this old time herb that has been used to cure everything for centuries. Terribly healthy, it is a palatable tea any time of the day. Combine it with mint tea.

Camomile

These flowers brew into a delicately flavored sunny yellow drink. Symbolizing "energy in adversity," camomile is an ancient herb dating back to the Egyptians. It is the tea they gave Peter Rabbit to ward off a possible cold after he raided Mr. McG's cabbage patch.

Quartet Blend Herb Tea

A combination of equal amounts of rose hip, hibiscus, peppermint and camomile, this delightful blend, delicious and hearty, is enjoyed by young and old alike. It has a full bodied flavor and a lovely wine red color that combines four beneficial and ancient herbs into a delectable fragrant drink.

MELISSA'S PUNCH

1 (6 oz.) can frozen lemonade
1 (8 oz.) can crushed pineapple
16 oz. frozen strawberries
2 or 3 quarts ginger ale
2 quarts lemon balm tea

First make the lemon balm (Melissa) tea. Steep 1/4 C. dried lemon balm leaves (or a handful fresh from the garden) in 1 quart briskly boiling water. Steep 10-15 minutes and strain. Add second quart of water. Blend together the lemonade, pineapple and strawberries (reserve a few to float as garnish). Combine the tea and fruit mixture.

This is an excellent punch with or without alcohol. It is nice to use two matching punchbowls, one with the above recipe and the other with a litre of sherry instead of the second quart of water. Pour over ice and garnish with lemon balm and strawberries. A ruffle of lemon balm around the base of the punch bowl is lovely.

MELISSA'S LEMON BALM LEMONADE

1½ C. sugar (or to taste)
1 C. water Grated peel of two lemons
1½ C. fresh squeezed lemon juice
3 C. lemon balm tea (see Melissa's Punch)
Crushed ice
Slices of lemon
Sprigs of lemon balm

Combine sugar, water and grated peel in saucepan, bring to a boil and simmer for 5 minutes. Strain and chill. Stir in lemon juice and lemon balm tea. Pour into a covered jar and refrigerate until ready to use. Fill tall glasses with crushed ice and 2 lemon slices. Add 1/4 C. lemon concentrate and fill with ice water. Mix and garnish each glass with a lemon balm sprig. Makes 10 to 12 servings.

GAZPACHO FIZZ

In a blender, combine 4 T. tomato puree, 1 scallion bulb with a little green left on, 1/2 medium rib celery, roughly chopped, 1 T. lemon juice and 1/4 tsp. celery seed. Blend to fine puree. Chill thoroughly. Pour into stemmed glass. Stir in 61/2 ounces of cold sparkling mineral water and garnish with cucumber stick or a leafy hollow stalk of lovage.

ROYAL WEDDING PUNCH

We first devised this wonderful recipe to celebrate the nation's bicentennial. We served it as "Patriot's Punch." No matter the occasion, it is always a hit.

1 qt. water, boiling briskly, poured over:
5 tsp. whole mint leaves
3 tsp. whole rosemary
2 tsp. whole sage
(Herbs may be fresh or dried)

Steep 10 min., strain and add:
1 C. sugar 1 small can frozen lemonade
4 tsp. instant tea
2 gal. cold water
1 qt. whiskey (optional)

Serve with sliced lemons stuck with whole cloves.

"and so they live happily ever after."

CAROLYNN'S RECEPTION PUNCH

1 (6 oz.) can frozen lemonade concentrate
1 large can pineapple juice, chilled (48 oz.)
2 bottles Sauterne, chilled
1 large bottle Champagne
Orange slices, Maraschino cherries, Alpine strawberries, herbs for garnish

Combine frozen lemonade concentrate and pineapple juice in punch bowl. Add one tray ice cubes or a block of ice made of lemonade. Just before serving pour in wines (or sparkling water for a non-alcoholic version). Makes 45 (3 oz.) servings.

To Health!
To Life!
To Love!

WARMING MIXER

For an evening treat on a cool day, mix equal parts of strong coffee and hot chocolate. Then top with whipped cream and a tiny sprinkle of nutmeg. Serve with crisp cookies.

WHITE GRAPE JUICE PUNCH

3 qts. white grape juice
3 qts. gingerale
Grated rind of six lemons
1½ C. water
1½ C. mixed fruit (pineapple, red or green seeded grapes, orange sections and strawberries)
3/4 C. thawed frozen lemon juice concentrate
1/2 C. frozen orange juice concentrate
12 - 16 drops peppermint flavoring
Mint sprigs as garnish

Chill juice and gingerale. Put lemon rind and water in small saucepan and boil, uncovered, until the liquid is reduced to half. Strain and chill. Put any combination fruits you like into a punch bowl. Pour grape juice and gingerale. Add lemon and orange juice concentrates, peppermint flavoring and lemon liquid. Add ice. Decorate with sprigs of mint. Yields 7 quarts, makes 40 servings.

PERCOLATOR PUNCH

Fill your percolator basket with cinnamon sticks, sugar and spices — and you have the tasty beginnings of a hot festive punch.

This non-alcoholic spiced punch is especially appropriate for winter weddings, church socials, and as an "extra" beverage where liquor is served.

2½ C. pineapple juice
1¼ C. water
2 C. cranberry juice
1 T. whole cloves
1/2 T. whole allspice
3 sticks cinnamon
1/4 tsp. salt
1/2 C. firmly packed brown sugar

Pour pineapple juice, water and cranberry juice into bottom of automatic 8 to 12 cup coffeemaker. Place remaining ingredients in basket. Set heat control on "strong" and complete perking cycle. Hold on "mild" setting. Serve hot in mugs or heatproof punch cups.

Here's to my mother-in-law's daughter,
And here's to her father-in-law's son;
And here's to the vows we've just taken,
And the life we've just begun!

SANGRIA

1 gal. sweet red wine
1 gal. diet Slice
Juice of a lemon
Ice
Fresh fruits (apples, oranges, and lots of sliced lemons)

Mix and serve.

COMFREY PARTY "SLUSH"

1 C. pineapple juice
1 box lime jello
3 - 6 leaves comfrey
2 - 3 qts. gingerale

Dissolve jello as directed. Chop comfrey leaves with pineapple juice in a blender. Strain. Combine with jello. Freeze. Serve by pouring gingerale over frozen comfrey cube in a large punchbowl. Stir frequently while serving.

"A toast to love and laughter
— Another to happily ever after!"

COLLEEN'S SLUSHIE

1 can orange juice, make as directed
1 can lemonade, make as directed
1 can whiskey sugar (optional)
Diet Slice

Blend and freeze. Scoop into glasses. Add diet Slice. Because of the alcohol it never freezes to a very hard state, so this can be made and kept in the freezer weeks in advance.

ROSEY ROSÉ PUNCH #1

6 fifths Rosé wine, chilled
2 quarts cranapple juice
1 pint rose water
2 C. light corn syrup
1 C. fresh lemon juice

Pour over ice ring made with roses in a large punch bowl. Add lemon slices and float rose petals to garnish. Makes 75 (3-oz.) servings.

ROSÉ PUNCH #2

6 fifths Rosé wine, chilled
2 qts. clear apple juice
2 C. light corn syrup
1 C. fresh lemon juice

Combine. Stir. Blend. Garnish with lemon slices and lemon balm. Makes 75 (3-oz.) servings.

ROSEMARY WEDDING WINE

1 gal. white wine (sherry, sauterne or chablis)
6 sprigs fresh rosemary
(or 2 T. dried rosemary in a muslin bag)

Steep rosemary in wine for a week before the wedding. Strain, chill and serve. This can also be done with apple juice to serve those who prefer.

Drink to me only with thine eyes,
And I will pledge with mine;
Or leave a kiss within the cup,
And I'll not look for wine.

DESSERTS and SWEETMEATS

POPPY SEED POUND CAKE

Poppy seeds are just what you'd think — a seed of that beautiful flower. We import almost all of our poppy seeds from the Netherlands, Australia and Turkey, but you can use the poppy seeds from your garden.

Poppy seeds have been a famous ingredient since Greek and Roman times, but nobody has ever topped central Europeans as users of these tiny blue seeds.

1 C. poppy seed
1/3 C. honey
1/4 C. water
1 C. butter or margarine, softened
1½ C. sugar
4 eggs, separated
1 C. sour cream
1 tsp. pure vanilla extract
2½ C. unsifted all-purpose flour
1 tsp. baking soda
1 tsp. salt
1 C. confectioner's sugar
4 tsp. cold water

In a small saucepan, cook poppy seed with honey and water for 5 minutes; cool.

In large mixing bowl, cream butter with sugar until light and fluffy. Stir in cooled poppy-seed mixture.

Add egg yolks, one at a time, beating well after each addition. Blend in sour cream and vanilla extract.

Sift together flour, soda and salt. Gradually add to poppy-seed mixture, beating well after each addition.

Beat egg whites until stiff peaks form. Fold into batter.

Pour batter into lightly greased and floured 10-inch tube pan. Bake in preheated 350° oven until done, about 1 hour and 15 minutes.

Cool in pan on a rack for 5 minutes. Remove cake from pan to a rack; cool completely. Blend confectioner's sugar with cold water until smooth. Spoon over cake. Makes 1 large cake.

MELISSA'S LEMON PUDDING DESSERT

Make one day ahead.
1½ C. flour
1½ sticks margarine (room temperature)
3/4 C. chopped pecans
1 large package cream cheese (room temperature)
1 C. powdered sugar
Cool Whip (9 oz. size), reserve half for topping
4 T. finely minced dried lemon balm
3 pkgs. lemon instant pudding
4½ C. milk

Mix flour, margarine and pecans and put in a 9x13 inch pan. Pat firmly in bottom of pan. Bake at 325° about 25-30 minutes. Cool.

Mix together cream cheese, lemon balm, powdered sugar and Cool Whip with mixer and spread over crust.

Mix pudding and milk until pudding is dissolved and spread over cream cheese mixture. Let set until firm. Then spread remainder of Cool Whip on top and sprinkle with chopped nuts.

SINFULLY SENSATIONAL ENGLISH TRIFLE

1 pint strawberries
1 two-layer sponge cake
1/2 lb. macaroons
6 T. strawberry jam
1 C. sherry
1 C. custard or pudding
1/2 pint heavy cream

Line a crystal trifle bowl with strawberries that have been sliced and lightly sugared. Place one layer of sponge cake in the bowl and spread strawberry jam over it. Cover with second layer of sponge cake. Add a layer of macaroons broken in pieces. Pour sherry over contents of bowl. Pour custard over all and chill until set. Shortly before serving, top with sweetened whipped cream and Alpine strawberries from your herb garden. This is an elegant dessert.

ROSEMARY'S DREAMINTS

Every party and wedding reception needs DreaMints, always a hit. Make them at your leisure; have them ready when you need them. There are many little soft molds available (the rose, leaf and bell are wedding favorites). This is a project even small children can enjoy. The DreaMints can be made in the wedding colors. They freeze well.

1 (8 oz.) pkg. cream cheese, softened
2-1 lb. boxes 10X sugar

Blend well, adding a little of the sugar to the cream cheese at a time. Add a few drops of your choice of flavoring (peppermint or lemon, etc.) and matching food coloring (pink or yellow, etc.) and continue kneading until well mixed, creamy and colorful. Roll into small balls, roll in a saucer of granulated sugar, press into the mint molds and arrange on flat plates.

PARTING PARTY PARCELS

2 Cardamon Seeds
Dill, anise and fennel seeds, a few each
1 piece crystallized ginger
2 candied mint leaves (or mint candies)
4 peanuts
Pinch of coconut (may be tinted)

Parcel out the above amounts onto a grape leaf or corn husk or maple leaf, as many as you need for your party. Secure with whole cloves or tie each packet with string. Bows and a cinnamon stick are optional. In India, similar after dinner treats are served after meals as an aid to digestion and to cleanse the palate. Keep the exquisite little packets on ice . . . with a smattering of rose petals! How elegant.

NANCY'S BEST SPICED NUTS

1 egg white, mixed with 1 tsp. water; beat until frothy
2 C. nuts, stir with egg white mixture until well coated
COMBINE:
  1/2 C. sugar
  3/4 tsp. cinnamon
  1/4 tsp. each, ground cloves, allspice and salt

Sprinkle over nuts and mix well. Spread coated nuts on an oiled shallow pan. Bake at 250°, stir every 20 minutes until coating hardens, about 1 hour. Use any kind of nuts; peanuts, pecans, walnuts, hazelnuts or cashews, etc.

HERBAL DIPS, NIBBLES and TIDBITS

LEMON BALM JELLY

To make the infusion or tea: Boil 3½ C. water and pour over a large handful of lemon balm. Steep until cool. Strain.

Measure:
3 C. infusion
4 C. granulated sugar
1 box Surejell
Juice of 1/2 lemon
1/2 capful of yellow food coloring

Combine and boil vigorously, stirring hard one minute. Count a minute that you cannot stir it down. Pour in jars and use paraffin to seal.

HOT OLIVE-CHEESE DIP

1 can (71/2-oz.) minced clams
2 (8-oz.) jars processed cheese spread
1 C. (1/4 pound) grated cheese, any kind
1/2 C. mayonnaise
1/8 tsp. garlic powder
1 tsp. Worcestershire sauce
1 C. chopped, pimiento-stuffed olives

Drain liquid from clams and reserve 1/4 cup. Combine reserved clam liquid, clams and remaining ingredients in 1½ quart casserole. Bake in hot oven (400°) 10 minutes. Stir and bake 5 to 10 minutes longer, or until bubbly. If desired, transfer to chafing dish and serve in miniature patty shells or serve as dip for corn and potato chips. (Makes about 5 cups)

ROSEMARY HOUSE PARTY SANDWICH SPREAD

1/4 lb. dried beef, soaked and drained
1/4 lb. sharp cheese
1/4 green pepper
Small onion
1 egg
1 C. tomato puree or soup

Grind dried beef, cheese, green pepper and onion. Add egg and puree or soup. Cook 5 minutes.

CHEESE BREAD

1/2 C. butter
1⅔ C. sugar (save 1/4 C. for top)
2 eggs
1 C. milk
2 C. flour
1 tsp. oregano
1/2 tsp. salt
3 tsp. baking powder
1 (8-oz.) pkg. cream cheese, cubed
1/2 C. walnuts
1/4 C. fresh orange juice
2 T. orange rind

Cream butter with sugar; add eggs and milk, flour, oregano, salt and baking powder; alternately fold in cubed cheese and walnuts. Bake at 350°, 40-50 minutes. While the bread is baking, mix the orange juice, 1/4 C. sugar and rind. Pour over bread, while hot.

HERBWICHES

1/2 loaf party rye, round and thin
1 (8-oz.) pkg. cream cheese, softened
2 generous handsfull culinary herbs
(ie. parsley, chives, mints, garlic chives, lemon balm, sage, burnet, tarragon, lovage, thyme, marjoram, basil, savory, rosemary or whatever you have)
10-12 red radishes
1 medium cucumber, scrubbed

Grate the unpeeled radishes and cucumbers. Drain. Chop, snip or mince the herbs finely (easily done in a food processor). Mix with the grated vegetables. Spread party rounds with softened cream cheese and top with a generous mound of the herb mixture. Serve these pretty open-faced sandwiches on a large tray, garnished with herbs.

If access to an herb garden is not possible, or if it is winter, use a bunch of parsley and celery or watercress tops from the supermarket with dried culinary herbs in any combination. They will be delicious, decorative and well received. We served these as Di's Diamonds for the royal wedding party.

SESAME SEED CHEDDAR STICKS

Sesame seeds should be sprinkled in a skillet and heated over moderate heat until golden if they are to be stirred into a mixture or showered over food.

1½ C. unsifted all-purpose flour
1/2 tsp. salt
2 T. sesame seeds
1 C. (4-oz.) shredded sharp cheddar cheese
1/2 C. butter or margarine
3 T. Worcestershire sauce
2 tsp. cold water

In a mixing bowl, combine flour, salt and sesame seeds. Cut in cheese and butter with pastry blender or two knives until crumbly. Sprinkle with Worcestershire sauce and water. Stir together with fork until mixture clings to side of bowl. Shape into a ball; handle lightly. On lightly floured board, roll out dough 1/4" thick. Cut into 3 x 1/2" strips; a zigzag cutter lends a nice touch. Place on ungreased baking sheets and bake in preheated 450° oven 8 to 10 minutes until golden. Remove to racks. Cool. Nice with drinks, soup or salad. Makes 3 dozen.

DEVILED EGGS

12 hard-cooked eggs
1 can boneless skinned sardines
2 T. finely minced green onion
1/2 tsp. savory
Juice of 1 lemon
1/2 tsp. Worcestershire sauce
Mayonnaise, if necessary
Ripe olives

Cool eggs quickly under cold running water. Shell and halve the long way. Remove the yolks carefully and mash. Drain and mash the sardines. Season them with minced onion, salt, lemon juice and Worcestershire sauce. Beat the mashed egg yolks into the sardine mixture and taste for seasoning. If the mixture needs binding, blend in a little mayonnaise. Using a spoon or knife, fill the egg whites with the sardine mixture through a pastry tube using the rosette attachment. Garnish each stuffed egg with slices of ripe olives and herbs.

SUSANNA'S CONVERSATION PIECE

1 (8-oz.) pkg. cream cheese
3/4 C. A.1. Steak Sauce

Put whipped cheese in shallow serving dish and pour A.1. liberally over it. *Looks like a chocolate sundae but makes a really tasty dip.*

DILLED OLIVES

1 clove garlic, crushed
1/2 tsp. dillweed
1 (9-oz.) jar large pimiento-stuffed olives

Add garlic and dillweed to liquid in olives. Shake well. Store in refrigerator at least several days to season.

MIDGET POPPY SEED TRIANGLES

A slick trick with a knife turns refrigerated rolls into these one-bite delights.

Separate 1 package refrigerated flaky rolls; cut each roll into quarters. Place quarters, an inch apart, on ungreased cookie sheet. Brush with 2 T. melted butter or margarine; sprinkle with 1 T. poppy seeds. Bake at 375° about 10 minutes. Serve hot. Makes 4 dozen.

LIPTAUER CHEESE

1 tsp. powdered mustard
2 T. warm water
1/2 C. butter or margarine, softened
1 (8-oz.) pkg. cream cheese, softened
1 T. minced onion
3 anchovy fillets, minced
1 T. capers, minced
1 T. caraway seed
Few twists freshly ground black pepper

In a cup, combine mustard and warm water. Let stand 10 mintues to develop flavor.

In a small mixing bowl, beat butter with electric mixer until soft. Add cream cheese, blending well.

Add mustard mixture along with remaining ingredients. Mix thoroughly. Serve as a spread with crackers. Makes 2 cups.

TERESA'S SAVORY SAUSAGES

1 lb. little tiny sausage links
(1 lb. equals approx. 50 links) (or slice Kielbasa)
1/2 C. current jelly
1½ T. lemon juice
1½ tsp. prepared mustard
1/2 C. chili sauce or 1/4 C. barbeque sauce
1 tsp. dry mustard
Dash of cayenne
1 large can cubed pineapple chunks, juice and fruit

Simmer slowly until sauce thickens and becomes almost a glaze. Reheat in a chafing dish to serve. Use toothpicks. (Make plenty, these are popular!)

Mark HOT dishes with red carnations or whole red peppers.

SCOTT'S STUFFED CLAMS

1 onion, minced
1 clove garlic, pressed
1 tsp. olive oil
1 C. minced clams with liquid
1 C. bread crumbs
1 tsp. lemon juice
2 T. white wine
1/4 C. grated parmesan cheese
1 T. minced parsley
1 tsp. oregano
Dash of salt and pepper

Saute onion and garlic in olive oil until golden brown. Add remaining ingredients, mix well. Stuff into clam shells. Bake at 350° for 10 minutes, serve.

PARSLEY BUTTER

2 sticks very soft butter
3/4 C. fresh parsley (cut fine)
1/4 tsp. grated onion (or more if you like)

Combine all ingredients. Place in refrigerator overnight. Soften before using spread. Can be kept for weeks, covered.

SAGE SANDWICH SPREAD

1 (8-oz.) pkg. cream cheese
1/2 lb. butter
1 T. onion juice
1 T. sage, fresh (or 1 tsp. dried)
1 T. celery salt
1 T. lemon juice

Beat all together until light and fluffy. Serve with hot biscuits or thin brown bread.

CAROL'S CRAB RING

1 tsp. unflavored gelatin
1/4 C. cold water
2 (8-oz.) pkgs. cream cheese, softened
2 T. cooking sherry
3/4 tsp. seasoned salt
1 (2-oz.) jar pimientos, sliced, drained
1 (6-oz.) pkg. frozen king crab meat, thawed, drained and cut up
1/8 tsp. ground black pepper
1/4 C. snipped parsley

Sprinkle gelatin over water to soften. Stir over hot water until smooth. Stir in next 5 ingredients and 2 T. parsley. Pour into a 3 C. ring mold. Refrigerate at least 4 hours or until set. Serve out of mold or on a plate. Garnish with remaining fresh parsley. Serve with crackers.

BUTTERY PARMESAN CRESCENTS with HERB BUTTER

2 (8-oz.) pkg. refrigerated crescent dinner rolls
1/2 C. (1 stick) butter, melted
(or use herb butter, recipe p. 160)
1/2 C. grated parmesan cheese

Preheat over to 375°. Unroll dough. Brush each piece gener-ously with melted herb butter; sprinkle with parmesan cheese. Roll up as package directs. Place on unbuttered baking sheet. Drizzle remaining herb butter over crescents; sprinkle with remaining cheese. Bake 13 to 15 minutes or until golden. Serve warm.

DILLED SALMON DIP

A Russian classic and easy!

1 (16-oz.) can red salmon
1/2 C. sliced green onions
1/4 C. chopped dill, fresh
1 C. dairy sour cream
2 T. white wine
1/8 tsp. black pepper

Drain red salmon well. Remove skin and bones and discard. Flake fish in small bowl. Add green onions and chopped dill. Toss to mix.

Heat dairy sour cream in top of chafing dish over flame until warm. Stir in salmon mixture, white wine and black pepper.

Place boiling water in bottom of chafing dish; set dish over flame. Put top over bottom to keep dip hot for serving. Serve as a dip. Makes 3 cups.

YOGURT HERB DIP with CRUDITES

2 tsp. instant dried onion
1/4 C. water, warm
2 C. yogurt
1/2 C. mayonnaise
2 T. dried parsley flakes
4 T. dried dillweed
1½ tsp. seasoned salt (Jane's is good)
1 tsp. lemon juice

Soften onion, parsley and dillweed in the water for 10 minutes. Combine all ingredients. Chill several hours before serving. Make 5 cups.

CRUDITES: Raw carrot sticks, celery sticks, cauliflowerettes, zucchini slices, cherry tomatoes, cucumber spears, eggplant fingers, raw mushrooms, radishes, broccoli buds, whole green beans, sweet red pepper strips, string beans, asparagus spears, summer squash chunks or snowpeas. Make your crisp fresh vegetable platter as colorful as possible.

MEGA EASY DIP

1 jar French dressing
1 (8-oz.) pkg. cream cheese

Mix dressing into cream cheese until it tastes good!

DILLY DIP

1 C. sour cream
2/3 C. mayonnaise
Grate a little onion
1 T. Bon Appetit
1 T. dillweed

Combine all ingredients. Mix well.

MARJORIE'S PINEAPPLE DIP

1 (16 oz.) cream cheese, softened
8 oz. crushed pineapple, drained
2 T. green onions include tops, chopped
1/2 C. green pepper, chopped
2 T. seasoned salt
2 C. pecans, chopped

Combine cheese and pineapple in a mixer. Stir in onion, green pepper, salt and one half of the pecans. Roll into a ball or a log or fill a scooped out fresh pineapple half. Roll remaining pecans on top.

TISH'S CRAB DIP

1 (3-oz.) pkg. cream cheese
1/3 C. mayonnaise
3 T. ketchup
1 T. grated onion (best if fresh, can substitute onion powder not onion salt)
1 small can crab meat, rinsed and drained

Mix all ingredients. Add a heaping teaspoon or more sour cream to achieve a thinner consistency. Let sit for 2 hours in refrigerator before serving. Note: To vary this already excellent, easy dip, add finely chopped spring onions or green pepper — or both.

For neat and tidy plates, make your finicky guests happy by serving small individual cups of herb dip. Easy to handle at buffets, it allows for individual convenience and neatness. Garnish each cuplet with an herb, alike or different. Serve with crisp veggies or crackers.

EDIBLE FLOWERS for FUN and FLAVOR

EDIBLE FLOWERS

EDIBLE FLOWERS, after centuries of neglect, are finally taking the world by storm. Since the supermarkets do not handle such perishables, these lovely additions to our cuisine have disappeared from our tables. Learn what's edible from your garden then plan to use it at your bridal party. Most florist flowers are sprayed, avoid them. There is nothing lovelier than fresh purple lilacs tossed in with a green salad or chicken salad served in bright pink tulip cups. Or try red rose petal sandwiches on white bread, steam daylily buds as a special vegetable or serve violet pinwheel sandwiches, always a hit.

HERBS — Eat the flowers and leaves, use them as seasonings or as garnishes liberally. Any of the following will dress your party: Angelica, borage, burnet, calendula or pot marigold, camomile, capers, catnip, chives, clary sage, costmary, dill, fennel, hyssop, lavender, lemon balm, marjoram, mignonette, mints of all kinds, oregano, rosemary (especially the flowers, when available), rue (pretty, but can be bitter), saffron, sage, tansy, thyme, sweet woodruff and yarrow (for a love that lasts), and violets, of course.

Don't overlook the power of flowers when you entertain. This ancient medieval practice is the latest thing in cookery and now is featured everywhere in posh restaurants. Use them as centerpieces, floating in drinking water, for garnishing plates and platters lavishly and to eat. Whether or not your guests are tempted to nibble on your flowers, use them anyway . . . with herbs, of course. Here's a long list for you to consider. Use only unsprayed flowers, well washed, covered with plastic, and conditioned under refrigeration.

Love note

For a most romantic touch — spike the white wine punch with delicate violet blossoms. These signs of spring will make your heart sing, floating in the punchbowl or waiting in empty glasses.

SOME EDIBLE FLOWERS

Acacia flowers, golden yellow
Apple buds and blossoms, pretty pink
Banana blossoms, if you have any
Borage, bright blue stars
Broom, Scotch broom, in gold
Carnations and their cousins, the "pinks"
Chrysanthemums
Clovers, assorted sizes and colors
Cornflowers or batchelor buttons
Cowslips, also known as Primroses
Daisies, they won't tell
Dandelion, flowers, leaves and root
Daylilies, my favorite (including Tiger Lilies)
Elderflowers, for beauty
Hawthorne, blossoms or berries
Hollyhocks, to stuff
Honeysuckle, symbol of fraternal love
Hyacinth, for fragrance
Jasmine, more fragrance
Johnny-jump-ups, Shakespeare's "heartsease"
Lemon, lime or orange blossoms
Lilacs in many colors
Lotus, exotic fare
Mallows, all the many mallows
Marigolds, especially the lemon scented
Nasturtiums, in brilliant colors
Orchids, yes, orchids strewn lavishly on foods and in drinks in Hawaii
Pansies, "that's for thoughts"
Passion flowers, they last but a day
Peony, petals or whole voluptuous blooms
Poppies
Roses, the most lovesome flowers for weddings, all kinds, and
Rosehips, too
Squash blossoms, all varieties
Snapdragons
Sunflowers, another daisy
Thistles, pretty but handle carefully
Tulips, in delightful colors
Violets
Wisteria, abundant in May
Yucca, pretty enough for a bride's bouquet

HOW TO CANDY HERBS AND FLOWERS

Use mint leaves, fresh lavender flower spikes, violet flowers, rose petals, coriander seeds, borage blossoms. Wash herbs of your choice and wrap in terry toweling then place in refrigerator to crisp and dry.

1 egg white, beat until frothy
food coloring
1 C. granulated sugar

Dip your herb in the beaten egg white (or colored egg white). Cover both sides carefully with sugar. Set aside to dry. This may take up to two weeks depending upon humidity. Use wax paper covered cookie sheets as egg white will glue itself to anything else. Don't even attempt to remove flower calyxes or you will have only petals. These will be the hit of your party, especially the lavender spike nibbles. Use as garnishes, favors or to decorate a pretty country look cake with snowy white icing.

Lavender grey, lavender blue,
Perfume wrapt in the sky's own hue;
Lavender blue, lavender grey,
Love in memory lives alway.

Lavender grey, lavender blue,
Sweet is remembrance if love be true;
Lavender blue, lavender grey
Sweeter methinks, is the love of today.

Lady Lindsay

LAVENDER STICKS

12 stalks fresh lavender flowers
1 egg white, beat until frothy
1/2 C. granulated sugar

Dip the lavender sprigs (flowers only) in egg whites then roll in or dust on the sugar. Air dry on waxed paper. Makes a dozen nibbles.

STUFFED NASTURTIUMS

1 C. (8 oz.) cream cheese
1/4 C. nuts, chopped
1/4 C. grated carrots
1 T. finely minced green pepper
3 T. mayonnaise
2 tsp. basil, parsley, dill, etc.
(or 2 T. chives, cucumber and green onion, minced)
1½ doz. brilliant Nasturtium blossoms

Soften cream cheese with mayonnaise, add other ingredients. Roll in balls and fit into washed nasturtium flowers. Top with a bit of chives or any edible blossom. Ring platter with round bright green nasturtium leaves. Or serve as individual salad garnishes, each on a leaf or two.

SALAD aFLEUR

2 heads of assorted greens
red leaf lettuce, endive
Edible flowers of your choice (see list)
Chopped parsley, chopped burnet and chopped chives for additional flavor

Wash and crisp lettuce by rolling it in clean dry toweling. Do the same with the flowers. Use flowers from an unsprayed garden. Arrange the bed of greens on a large platter, then sprinkle with the colorful flowers. Keep covered with plastic wrap and refrigerate until ready to serve. Serve with Poppy Seed Dressing.

POPPY SEED DRESSING

1/3 C. lemon juice
2/3 C. light corn syrup
1/4 C. salad oil
1 T. poppy seed
1/8 tsp. salt

Shake vigorously to blend. Makes 1½ cups.

VIOLET JELLY

Collect very small pretty glasses to use this as a decorative favor. For a rich violet color, pick lots of violets in season. The more flowers you steep, the richer the purple color. It is a jewel-like garnish for any party plate.

To make: fill a quart jar with violet blossoms; cover with boiling water. Steep for 24 hours. Strain. To 2 cups of this liquid, add the juice of 1 lemon and 1 box of Sure Jel. Bring to a boil and add 4 cups of sugar. Bring again to a boil and boil hard for 1 minute. Ladle into jars. Seal with paraffin or freeze.

VIOLET PINWHEELS

Be sure to serve these pretty-as-a-picture sandwiches whenever violets are in bloom. It is truly a showpiece. It also makes a delicious tea party.

Use softened cream cheese, mix with minced fresh chives, thyme, parsley, lemon balm and/or tarragon. Spread on thin-sliced white bread. Cover with violets and roll up. Refrigerate each roll, wrapped in a paper towel, in a covered dish.

To serve, cut pinwheels with a scissors and place on a silver tray with lace paper doilies. Top each little pinwheel with a fresh violet blossom and serve immediately.

Blue Violets symbolize Faithfulness.
Dame Violets for Watchfulness.
Sweet Violets are for Modesty.
Yellow Violets stand for Rural Happiness.

SOURCES

SOURCES

FRESH CUT HERBS

(Write First for Current Information)

Vali Hai Herbs
Mark Dayley
979 W. Bannock Street
Boise, ID 83702 — (208) 376-HERB

Bay Laurel Farm
Glory H. Condon
West Garzas Road
Carmel Valley, CA 93924 — (408) 659-2913

Paradise Farms (for edible flowers)
Pam and Jay North
Box 436
Summerland, CA 93067 — (805) 684-9468

Fox Hill Farm
Marilyn Hampstead
444 W. Michigan Avenue, Box 9
Parma, MI 49269 — (517) 531-3179

Northhaven Farm
Sally Watts
2230 Brownsboro Highway
Eagle Point, OR 97524 — (503) 826-7832

Glie Farms
The Bronx, NY (212) 731-2130
Boston, MA (617) 483-7548
Chicago, IL (312) 263-6710
Philadelphia, PA (215) 925-7548

Taylor's Herb Garden
Jean Langley
1535 Lone Oak Road
Vista, CA 92083 — (602) 992-7967

Herb Gathering, Inc.
Paula A. Winchester
5742 Kenwood
Kansas City, MO 64110 — (816) 523-2653

OTHER ACCESSORIES

Arts and Flowers of Cider Hill Farm

Gary Milek
R.R. #1, Box 1066
Windsor, VT 05089

Write to Gary to order his symbolic wedding herb print (page 103) to frame or to use as notepapers. The notecards are very handy.

Maid of Scandinavia

3244 Raleigh Avenue
Minneapolis, MN 55416

For heart shaped doilies, tier cake pans, wedding bells galore, strings of pearls and a bride's "lucky sixpence" for her shoe, write for a wedding catalog.

Smithsonian Institute

Dept. 0006
Washington, DC 20073-0006

Write for wonderful die-cut bride paper doll wedding cards.

Nature's Jewelry

639 Massachusetts Ave.
P.O. Box 9132
Cambridge, MA 02139

For gold or silver herb jewelry — parsley, four leaf clovers and others.

The Rosemary House, Inc.

120 S. Market Street
Mechanicsburg, PA 17055
(717) 697-5111

For mint molds, extracts, wedding rice, and other helpful herbal items, such as wreath or herbal craft supplies, "The Fairy" roses, Flower-Dri, "Rosemary for Remembrance" sampler to embroider, etc. Catalog $2.00.

"One leaf for fame,
And one for wealth,
One for a faithful lover,
And one to bring glorious health."

"Everything Grows with Love."

INDEX AND RECIPE INDEX

GENERAL INDEX

RECIPE INDEX

POSTLUDE

If all this seems like much ado about "I do" bear in mind the awesome significance of a wedding, it's a lifetime commitment.

Such a quantum leap forward pours excess adrenalin into the body, all of it demanding to be put to good use. The many extra little herbal projects in *THE BRIDE'S HERBAL* will satisfy these needs. Given plenty of time, you can express yourself by personally designing your wedding with careful attention to all details.

As the date approaches and excitement mounts, the pace quickens. Touched by love, there's much to be said for making bows, stuffing baskets with herb arrangements, gluing pressed herbs on placecards, folding fancy flared napkins, freezing pretty ice rings of herbs for the parties.

Each and every idea scratched off endless lists well in advance means precious last minute time to enjoy your party and play along with your guests. Pamper yourself! Then don your wedding gown and join your families and friends in all the justified and carefree festivities.

A word of caution: Although you can do it all by yourself if you want to, I would advise against such folly. There are enough ideas in *THE BRIDE'S HERBAL* to keep a dozen brides and their families and friends busy planning their weddings and peripheral parties. And don't forget the anniversaries to come when *THE BRIDE'S HERBAL* will prove indispensable.

Be selective. Don't hesitate to parcel out projects to talented friends or professionals. Smart planning and detailed lists, teamwork and cooperation assures you a picture perfect day to remember.

When you are at last altar bound to the jubilant strains of Wagner, radiantly beautiful, carrying a bouquet redolent of fragrant herbs, think of their ancient symbolism. Herbs don't shout, they whisper . . . a romantic sonnet that will sustain you for a lifetime of wedded bliss.

A herbal wedding will do just that. The secret lies in good planning along with a little effort and simple ingenuity using herbs. Herbs make all the difference in the world.

Love suffereth long,
and is kind ; Love envieth
not ; Love vaunteth not
itself, is not puffed-up, doth
not behave itself unseemly,
seeketh not her own, is not
easily provoked, thinketh no
evil ; Rejoiceth not in
iniquity, but rejoiceth in the
truth ; Beareth all things,
believeth all things, hopeth
all things, endureth all
things.
Love never faileth.
And now abideth faith, hope,
love, these three ;
But the greatest of these
is love.

1 Corinthians 13th chapter